EARLY CHILDHOOD EDUCATION SERIES

Leslie R. Williams, Editor
Millie Almy, Senior Advisor

Advisory Board: Barbara T. Bowman, Harriet K. Cuffaro, Doris Fromberg, Celia Genishi, Alice Sterling Honig, Elizabeth Jones, Gwen Morgan, David Weikart

The Land of Counterpane

When I was sick and lay a-bed
I had two pillows at my head
And all my toys beside me lay
To keep me happy all the day.

And sometimes for an hour or so
I watched my leaden soldiers go,
With different uniforms and drills,
Among the bed-clothes, through the hills:

And sometimes sent my ships in fleets
All up and down among the sheets;
Or brought my trees and houses out,
And planted cities all about.

I was the giant great and still
That sits upon the pillow-hill,
And sees before him, dale and plain
The pleasant land of counterpane.

Robert Louis Stevenson
A Child's Garden of Verses

The War Play Dilemma
BALANCING NEEDS AND VALUES IN THE EARLY CHILDHOOD CLASSROOM

Nancy Carlsson-Paige

and

Diane E. Levin

Teachers College, Columbia University
New York and London

Published by Teachers College Press, 1234 Amsterdam Avenue,
New York, NY 10027

Library of Congress Cataloging-in-Publication Data

Carlsson-Paige, Nancy.
  The war play dilemma.

  (Early childhood education series)
  Bibliography: p.
  Includes index.
  1. Play—United States.   2. Children and war—
United States.   3. Toys—United States—Psychological
aspects.   4. Child development—United States.
5. Teacher-student relationships—United States.
I. Levin, Diane E.   II. Title.   III. Series.
LB1137.C29   1987   155.4'18   87-7086

ISBN 0-8077-2875-6

Manufactured in the United States of America

92 91 90 89   2 3 4 5 6

Contents

Foreword

Educators and parents are beginning to confront an epidemic of growing proportions: the proliferation of high-tech war toys that encourage children to simulate administering painless death to their playmates and other victims without thought or imagination. War toys, as the authors of *The War Play Dilemma* indicate, have been with us for a long time. But in contemporary American society, the deregulation of violence on commercial television and the pandering by toy companies to the appetites of children stimulated by feature-film and television images of sadistic killers have combined to create a new dilemma for teachers and parents that Nancy Carlsson-Paige and Diane Levin address in this book.

Teachers, to whom the authors are speaking most directly, share responsibility for guiding the development of children and representing creative and civilized cultural values. This task, never an easy one, has become more difficult as the culture has moved toward worshipping violence and mass-produced toys have reduced the repertoire of possibilities for contending with the human complexities of good and evil, friendship and enmity, power and helplessness to the bloodless murder of designated bad guys by stereotypic robot (or robot-like) killer-heroes.

War toys may play an inevitable role, the authors realize, in the developmental processes by which boys, and to a lesser extent girls, gain a sense of mastery over conflicts related to love and hate, and may also be instrumental in introducing social and political values. However, toys that leave nothing to imagination lend themselves only to simple imitation. At best, they contribute little that is constructive from a developmental standpoint; at worst, they sanction thoughtless violence and hatred toward whatever objects the mass culture designates as alien or "other."

The war toy problem looms large in the classroom because it impedes the capacity of teachers to carry out their responsibility for the education of children, but in truth it is really only a symptom of the larger disease of militarism in American society. Militarism is more than war. It is a prevailing cultural attitude that supports the proliferation and glorification of weaponry and emphasizes violent solutions to political differences between ethnic or national groups. Militarism is supported by ideologies of enmity that find all fault in the adversary and discourage national self-criticism or the acknowledgment of self-responsibility for current international conflicts and tensions.

In the America of the 1980s, militarism is enormously profitable for many institutions. Some of them—defense contractors, universities engaging in military research, consulting firms, high-technology laboratories—benefit directly, while others gain their advantage from the economic and moral deregulation that inevitably accompanies a militaristic ethos. Among these latter are the manufacturers of war toys. Executives of a major toy company were recently approached by two entrepreneurs who had an ingenious idea for a war game that proposed nonviolent solutions to conflict. Some of the executives were excited by the project, but the proposal was turned down by top management, which thought it not likely to be sufficiently profitable without the violent element. In rejecting the proposal the executives argued that it was not the company's responsibility to reform the appetites of American children.

As the authors of *The War Play Dilemma* show clearly, the options of teachers in the classroom are limited. Efforts to prohibit toys for which the appetites of children have been commercially whetted cannot succeed. They have recommended the only viable path open to teachers: to permit only safe toys in the classroom and to participate with children in the play itself in order to facilitate specific developmental processes. Teachers who follow this course may have some chance of enabling children to think more complexly, use their imaginations, learn to identify with an adversary's humanity, interfere with sex-role stereotyping, and find alternatives to violence in the negotiation of conflicts in human relationships.

The public policy implications of *The War Play Dilemma* are as important as its educational recommendations. Solutions to the problems presented here can come only from the reform of the social institutions whose decisions affect the mental lives of children. In particular we may hope that this book will inspire teachers, parents, and all the rest of us who are concerned with the emotional and ethical development of children to take a stand against the pandering to naked political violence that modern war toys represent. The struggle to develop political and corporate self-responsibility in the institutions that affect the education of children must take place outside the classroom. In a democracy this is everyone's job.

John E. Mack, M.D.
March 1987

Acknowledgments

It is the parents and teachers of young children who hold collective responsibility for the development of our interest in the topic of children's war play. They forced it upon us over and over again as an issue of concern. At first we didn't listen very carefully, but you can hear the same thing from different people just so many times before realizing that it has to be taken seriously. As we began to look at the issue more closely, we realized the significance of what these adults were saying and why they had expressed their concern with such persistence. So our first thanks go to all of the parents and teachers who led us into the maze of the war play dilemma.

We wish to thank the parents and teachers at the four preschool and daycare centers who took the time to complete our questionnaires so thoughtfully, and the many other parents and educators who willingly expressed their ideas and feelings in interviews.

Valuable feedback on various drafts of the manuscript played an important role in helping us refine how the ideas are presented in this book. For their help, we thank Gary Goldstein, Jay Jones, Mieko Kamii, and Karen Worth. We also appreciate the contributions of Susan Cohen and Gretchen Hensel Hall who, in their roles as research assistants, showed a willingness to do just about anything we asked them to, in order to help push the project along.

For reducing our faculty responsibilities in order to allow time for us to do this work and for providing environments in which our work has always been valued, we thank Lesley College and Wheelock College.

The research and writing that have gone into this book represent a truly collaborative endeavor between the authors. To each other we wish to express warmth and appreciation for the rich and fulfilling experience that this project has provided.

The basis for all of the ideas in this book is our experience with children. We are grateful to all of the children who accepted our presence in their classrooms, ignored our notebooks and tape recorders, and just went on playing. Thanks also go to the many others who answered our questions about their play so freely, and to Andrew McLellan for sharing his Christmas list. To our own children—"Spiderman," his costume designer, and "Monster Frog"—who helped us to appreciate more deeply the power of play in children's lives, we express special gratitude. It is to all of these children that this book is dedicated.

The War Play Dilemma:
BALANCING NEEDS AND VALUES IN THE EARLY CHILDHOOD CLASSROOM

To what extent people draw their ideas from fiction is disputable. Personally I believe that most people are influenced far more than they would care to admit by novels, serial stories, films and so forth, and that from this point of view the worst books are often the most important, because they are usually the ones that are read earliest in life. It is probable that many people who would consider themselves extremely sophisticated and "advanced" are actually carrying through life an imaginative background which they acquired in childhood. . . .

George Orwell
Boys' Weeklies (1946)

CHAPTER 1

Approaching the War Play Dilemma

It is recess time. Three 4-year-old boys race up the climbing structure and jump off, arms straight above their heads. They run over to the giant tire embedded in the sand and crawl inside. One picks up a stick and points it toward other children who are playing; the other two point their fingers. They squint their eyes and pop their lips. They leap out, race across the playground, fists and arms clenched. They knock over a smaller child but don't notice. The teacher walks over and says something to them. They walk away, run back up the structure, point their fingers again, and dive off. One child makes a karate chop in mid-air and lands partly on top of a child who is digging in the sand below. All three run back to the giant tire—one boys pulls a "G.I. Joe" doll out of his pocket.

"I'm concerned about war play in my classroom. It really upsets me to see children pretending to shoot and kill people. Some children seem so obsessed with it that it's hard to stop them. I don't know if I should let the children play this way or if they need to for some reason. I don't want to teach them that violence is acceptable."

"My son likes to watch television in the afternoons. His favorite shows are 'He-Man' and 'Rambo.' He pretends he's one of these characters a lot of the time. He wants the He-Man and Rambo dolls and all the things that come with them to play with. The other day we were at the park. My son climbed the slide and pushed another child. I told him he couldn't do that, that it's not right to hurt other children. He said, 'I didn't do it, He-Man did it.' I don't like any of these characters or the way he's so preoccupied with them."

The preceding vignette and the quotes from two adults express a dilemma that many teachers and parents are currently voicing. They see that young children often have a compelling interest in war and weapons play,[1] yet they worry about the concepts and values this play might be teaching. They are trying to decide how they should respond to such play and what the effects of different responses might be on children's development and learning.

War play has been a topic of interest and debate among early-childhood educators and parents for many years. Questions about how the play relates to childhood play and learning in general and about how teachers and parents should respond to it have often been asked (Bettelheim, 1967; Biber, Murphy, Woodcock, & Black, 1942; Feinberg, 1973, 1975; Pitcher & Prelinger, 1969). One early-childhood educator who has been in the field for almost fifty years told us that during World War II, as children acted out what they had heard about the war, there were parents and teachers who expressed concern about the values this play might be teaching children. Numerous teachers and school directors have told us that toy guns and war play have always been frequent topics of discussion among staff. They say that discussions often focus on deciding what approach to take to the play, how to interpret a school's ban on guns (e.g., "What if children use fingers as guns?" or, "What if children say 'Pow' or 'You're dead' with no evidence of an imaginary or toy weapon?"), or how to manage war-related play in the classroom.

Recently, however, war play has become the focus of increasing attention and debate. Numerous articles have appeared in professional journals and the popular press on the subject of children's war and weapons play, its origins and possible effects (Denison, 1985; Engel-hardt, 1986; Kostelnik, Whiren, & Stein, 1986; MacMaster, 1986; Ra-posa, 1986; Schneiderman & Sousa, 1986; Witkowsky, 1986; Wolf, 1984). Often, strong positions either in favor of allowing or of banning the play are adopted by the authors.

In an effort to learn more about the war and weapons play that children are currently engaging in, and the nature of parents' and educators' attitudes and questions about it, we have been collecting data through both questionnaires and in-depth interviews with a wide range of parents and teachers. We have also observed children and

---

[1]The phrase *war and weapons play* is used throughout as a generic term to refer to all forms of combat play in which children engage, including theme play such as "Star Wars," "Rambo," "G.I. Joe," "He-Man," and "Transformers"; and play with real and pretend weapons and superhero and action figures.

interviewed several about their play (see Appendix I, "Sample Questionnaires and Summary of Responses"). While war play was not a matter of deep concern to all of the adults we contacted, it was a topic about which, when mentioned, everyone wanted to talk. Moreover, the responses of many parents and teachers indicated that war play was a topic that engendered feelings of ambivalence, helplessness, and concern.

Where to Begin

In this book, we address the desire expressed by many teachers and parents for a better understanding of war play and its relationship to children's development and learning, so that decisions about how to respond to the play can be made. We look at why so many children seem to be deeply interested in war and weapons play, what the possible effects of such play might be on children's developing attitudes and values, how current societal factors might be influencing the play, and possible adult roles and responsibilities with respect to the play.

We take as our starting point the belief that a major goal of our work with children is to help them grow up to become citizens who can live peacefully in the world—citizens who seek alternatives to violence in resolving conflicts among people and who have a sense of respect and caring for others. At the same time, we also believe that we have a responsibility to respond to the needs and interests of individual children in ways that are appropriate to their experience and level of development.

There is almost no research on the subject of war play, either in terms of its nature and the extent to which children are involved in it or in terms of how it affects children's development and learning. Such research is very much needed. At the same time, the concerns and confusion that many educators and parents are expressing cannot wait. We need to find ways to understand and respond to what is currently happening with children's war play, and we can best do this based on what we currently know.

What we attempt to do here is to combine related child development and political socialization theory and research with the practical experiences of the many parents, teachers, and children with whom we have worked, in order to bring some clarity to the issues underlying the war play dilemma. We share the concern expressed by many adults that today's children are exposed to too much violence too early. We also believe that adults have a crucial role to play in affecting the society in which children are growing up so that war play will not always be so pressing an issue. However, we feel that a solution has to be found that takes into account that children are being exposed to this violence. Here we will be considering how adults can respond to children's needs and their own needs in the world as it exists today, rather than in the ideal world we would like to see for our children.

The Choice Facing Teachers

Should war play be allowed, or should it be banned? This question is often debated by adults who work or live with young children. Generally, how one answers this question depends on which of two fundamentally different points of view about war play one chooses to take. One view holds that children should be allowed to engage in war play because it meets certain of their developmental needs (Kostelnik et al., 1986; Wolf, 1984). The other view argues that children should not be allowed to engage in war play because it teaches them attitudes of violence and militarism[2] (Schneiderman & Sousa, 1986; Simpson, 1985). The developmental view focuses primarily on the needs of children and how war play meets these needs, rather than on the relationship this play might have to real-world violence. The sociopolitical view focuses primarily on the relationship of children's war play to real-world violence rather than on the developmental needs that the play might be meeting.

The words of two teachers we interviewed illustrate the contrast between the developmental and the sociopolitical sides of the war play debate:

"I don't know enough about why children need to play this way, but I see that they do and I respect that. If children come into my classroom and they want to play in a certain way, then I accept that as expressing a legitimate need. I think the play is primarily about power. Children are learning about how it feels to be powerful, because, of course, they're not. But in war play they can act out powerful roles, they can pretend to have supernatural powers and use powerful pretend props that make them

---

[2]The words *militarism* and *militaristic* are used in this book to connote the glorification of war and fighting as well as the encouragement and glamorization of attitudes of hostility, belligerence, and combativeness.

feel strong. Children also have a lot of aggressive feelings which this kind of play allows them to express safely. These feelings are part of every child, and I don't want to tell children that they have to leave them at the school door. If I did this I wouldn't be valuing them as whole people."

"I think that allowing children to engage in war play undermines all the values we want to teach them. The TV characters they bring into this play are terrible models for children—they always hurt people, they're always fighting, they deal with all conflict by violence, and they are very sexist. What are we teaching when we allow this play? Do we want to raise children who learn that we kill people when they're bad or when we don't agree with them? I want to teach children to use words and express their feelings when there's conflict; to try to see the other person's point of view in a disagreement. I want to teach children to resolve differences in a nonviolent way and in a caring way. I don't feel that it is okay to pretend that someone is getting hurt. I believe that society is promoting the kind of play in children that develops a war mentality, and as teachers we have a responsibility to sabotage it."

Both of these teachers' arguments seem to have some common-sense validity; at the same time, the conclusions that grow out of each seem to be contradictory. Many of the teachers we interviewed adhered to one of the two sides of the debate, but many fell in between, seeing both points of view and expressing a general dilemma about what their approach to war play should be in their classrooms. They are asking, If children need to play at war and I therefore allow the play, am I also teaching attitudes of violence? or, If war play teaches children a militaristic view of the world and I therefore ban the play, am I robbing children of an important vehicle for working on developmental issues? And some teachers, who had been strong adherents to one or the other side of the debate in the past, were also beginning to question their approach.

Many teachers seem to be experiencing the war play dilemma more acutely than in the past and as a result are finding themselves taking a closer look at both sides of the debate. They are asking if there is some way to resolve the war play dilemma as they are currently experiencing it, a way of meeting many children's apparent need to engage in war play while at the same time insuring that the play is not teaching children attitudes of violence and militarism.

CHAPTER 2

The Current Situation

What is the nature of the concerns being expressed by parents and teachers? Why has war play become the focus of so much discussion and concern? Is something happening that has caused the debate among adults to heighten now? Several factors seem to be upsetting the equilibrium adults felt about their approaches to war play in the past.

Tensions in Teacher-Child Relationships

First, many teachers are finding that the approaches they have always taken to war play in their classrooms are no longer working or are not working as well as they once did. Regardless of whether they have allowed or banned war play, these teachers are saying that it has recently become an issue of increasing tension and struggle with children. We heard this from teachers of children as young as 2 years old.

Many of those who adhere to the sociopolitical view and therefore have always banned the play are saying banning no longer works. Some say they have to repeat their "no guns in school" rule with increasing frequency. As one such teacher told us,

> "I have taught for 15 years and always had the policy that children put their real or pretend guns in their pocket because 'we can't use our guns at school, they can hurt people.' We want them to know that even pretending to hurt others is not okay. I still have the rule . . . but must state it two or three times as often as a few years ago. I'm really losing my patience."

And one school director, who also has been in the field for many years, told us,

"I don't envy the parents and teachers of today's children. I am
a pacifist, and, when I was the parent of a young child and first
started teaching, I didn't permit war or weapons play at home
or school. Most children accepted this easily. Now, my son
shares my political attitudes. He has been trying to prevent war
play in his home with his 6-year-old son. He tells me that it's a
constant struggle. All of his child's environment—his friends,
the toys they play with, television programs, and ads—is permeated with aggression and violence which keep erupting in
his play. The teachers and many of the parents at my school
tell me the same thing. They don't know what to do in or out
of the classroom to stop the play."

Other teachers who ban war play describe children doing such things
as sneaking under the slide to pull out a gun or finding increasingly
ingenious ways of getting around the "no guns or superheroes in
school" rule.

Those teachers who have allowed the play, even within strict
limits (e.g., okay on the playground, but with no "real" guns), are
saying that the play is getting out of control and stretching their
management skills to new levels.

"I have always allowed a kind of war play in the dramatic play
area, without toy guns (we call them 'real guns'). I'm beginning
to question this. A child will bring in a toy 'laser' and ask if it's
okay because 'it's not a gun.' A group will get so involved in the
play that they zoom out of the block area pretending to shoot
everyone in the room. I have to devote so much of my energy to
explaining rules and controlling the play that I'm beginning to
wonder if I should ban it completely."

As teachers' continuous attempts to adapt their war play policies
meet with increasingly creative resistance from the children, teachers
are led to question their whole approach to war play. Sometimes they
become critical of parents who allow their children to watch violent
television and play with war-related toys. It has also led to disagreements among teachers who work together about the war play policies
they should adopt in their classroom or school.

Tensions in Parent-Child Relationships

The responses of parents to our questions revealed that teachers
were not alone in their current discomfort and confusion about war

play. Many parents of young children, especially boys, are saying that war play is an ongoing and growing source of tension between themselves and their children. Many describe a sense of being out of control or of resignation with respect to their ability to influence and/or limit their children's involvement in war play. Such views are often expressed these days by parents of adolescents (Winn, 1983) but are generally not voiced by parents of young children.

When we asked parents why they felt war play had recently become such an issue for themselves and their children, they often pointed to changes in society, television, and toys, which they saw as major sources of their concern. They said that they could not turn on the television, visit other children, or go to a supermarket, toy store, or playground with their children without encountering some reminder of war and weapons play. Often they pointed to the peer group at school as the origin of their children's interest in war play and sometimes blamed teachers for allowing the play in the school. They were concerned about such things as the degree of exposure to violence society now presents to their children, their children's insatiable desire for an endless array of war toys, and the diffuse aggression that they often observed in their children's play. Parents also said that war play was a topic that they are discussing with increasing frequency with their friends who have children and with their children's teachers.

The response of the parent of a 6-year-old boy reflects many of the issues expressed by parents:

> "Gary learned about war play in the neighborhood when he was about three. I tried to ban the violent TV shows and toys in our home, but his grandparents gave him a 'G.I. Joe' machine gun. We always have struggles at toy stores for more of those toys. And, when I ask him not to watch the TV shows at home, he'll watch them at a neighbor's. It all makes me feel I have no control . . . I'm afraid I end up getting 'out of control' myself. . . . I yell and get angry. This doesn't help. All of his friends do it. I feel I can't do anything about it. I don't know where to turn."

Several parents also described how the tension in their relationships with their children crept into their relationships with other adults. One mother of an 8-year-old boy who was "passionately" involved in war play described the following ongoing scenario between herself and her husband. It graphically illustrates the degree to which emotions, personal and political beliefs, and concerns for children all can contribute to the "dilemma" about war play many parents are experiencing.

"The struggle between my husband and myself about Jack's interest in war and gun play has been growing. Jack seems to be 'obsessed' with war play and play with guns. He spends endless hours making drawings of battle scenes, with detailed copies of military bombers, missiles, and guns of both the United States and Soviet Union, or of the make-believe characters he sees created on TV cartoons. He wants camouflage clothes, and he uses his allowance to buy guns and toys that are like the ones advertised on television. We will not buy these things for him, but he can do what he wants with his allowance.

"When Jack first expressed interest in guns, when he was 3 years old, my husband and I were in agreement that we would not allow guns in our home. We wanted Jack to learn from the start that guns and violence were offensive to us, even in 'play.' We were uncomfortable watching the play shooting and killing and felt we had a responsibility to teach our values to Jack.

"We have found it is very hard to hold to our position on this. Jack made guns out of anything—his finger, clay, paperclips. He kept asking for guns from grandparents and Santa Claus. Guns were the first thing he always went after at friends' houses. The attraction of the 'gun' seemed much more powerful than our explanations of why his friends could have guns but he couldn't. At my urging, we finally decided to give Jack a toy gun. We realized that we could not totally stop this play, even though we had tried. We were making it into a real power struggle with him. I guess I decided that one gun, used with careful limits and a lot of communication about our values, would be a better compromise. I guess I hoped that it would lead to a decrease in his interest in guns and war play, as it ceased being such a big issue between him and us.

"However, things didn't go as I had hoped. With time, Jack seemed to get more and more involved with the play until now it seems like one of his major interests. We gave in more and more but always with discomfort and ambivalence, especially on my husband's part. He never agreed with allowing the play but didn't have any very helpful ideas about what we should do, so he went along with me. We now are in real conflict. He is convinced we are creating a soldier and warmonger and is feeling trapped by Jack and me. I still feel that his play and war drawings tap into some basic needs Jack has, and I can't see treating this completely differently from how we respond to his other interests. I'm still not sure why it's such a passion for him and wonder if it points to some emotional needs that aren't being met. But, I also see he isn't an overly aggressive or mean child. He seems to care about others."

Changes in Play

A third factor that seems to be fueling the war play debate is that many educators, particularly those who have been working with children over a long period of time, have observed *changes in the quality and content of children's play, including war play.* Many of the adherents of the developmental view are worried that *war play is no longer meeting children's needs in the way it once did.* They say that the current war play of many children is repetitive; that many children seem to get stuck and repeat the same play behavior over and over, as if by rote, rather than elaborate their play over time. They describe children as assuming the roles of characters they have seen on television and often playing out scenes that resemble television scripts. Children's play scenarios often use simple static schemes and a lot of aimless running around combined with aggressive "macho" and stylized actions. Many children no longer seem to be in full charge of their play. As one daycare center director, who has worked with children for more than 30 years, told us,

> "The children's play is not as dimensional or breadthy as it used to be. They do the same thing over and over—they don't stick with it. They won't try something a lot of different ways; they'll try one thing and then walk away—I mean everybody. They kind of skim along. Some are still okay if you take the time to get them more breadthy, but you'd hope they'd do it themselves. They don't stick with any of it. It's like they keep changing the channels on television. I don't think of this as 'Things aren't like they used to be.' I have a real kernel of fear inside me about this stuff. Look at how little they are. What are they going to be like when they're twelve years old?"

Or, as another school director told us,

> "I got divorced when my son was 2 years old. From an early age he loved all kinds of weapons and superhero play. I always felt that he needed it—that it was providing him with a way to express his anger and to feel in control of his life. I figured

other children had their own needs that were met in the play. But now I watch the 'battle' play at my center and it really concerns me. The kids do the same things over and over; it doesn't seem to be getting anywhere. They often run around saying 'pow' or 'bang, bang' with no real purpose. It just doesn't feel right."

Some adherents of the sociopolitical view are also concerned about the changes in play, particularly what appears to them to be *an increase in the aggression and violence in children's play*. They say that the quantity of aggression and violence has increased dramatically and it seems to permeate more and more of all kinds of children's play. Many children are not distinguishing between pretending to hurt someone and actually hurting them; and when some children do hurt another child, they either do not realize it or resist taking responsibility for it. Finally, the characters they are modeling themselves after are increasingly of the militaristic type taken directly from television. In the words of one teacher of 3-year-olds,

"I do not permit war play in my classroom, but it sure feels like it's there. Some of the kids find ways to bring it into anything. One boy got red paint on his hands and went around threatening the other children with 'blood from where he was shot.' Another child, with no warning, started crashing into children [who were] playing ball, saying he was 'Rambo.' In the house area recently, three children tore the head off of the teddy bear. All they could tell me was that the bear was the 'bad guy.' They can't seem to get war play out of their minds."

In sum, educators holding either view are concerned because children's war play has become a source of tension in their relations with children. They say that children seem to be increasingly obsessed with the play; that it is harder to allow and manage, or ban; and that it is invading the curriculum in a way that is eroding the teachers' sense of control.

Changes in Television and Toys

Many of the comments from educators and parents we interviewed, regardless of whether they chose to allow or ban war play, pointed to concerns about the detrimental effects of television on children's play. This is not a new issue (Cohen, 1974; Doerkin, 1983; Group for the Advancement of Psychiatry, 1982; Rudolph & Cohen, 1984; Winn, 1983, 1985), but worries about it seem to be increasing.

This observation by adults points to a fourth factor that may help explain the current increase in debate about war play: *Violent television programming for children is increasing dramatically.* In September of 1985, the number of war-related television cartoons went from two to ten, and five more were planned for the fall of 1986. In one of the most popular current children's television shows, "Transformers," there is an average of eighty-three violent acts per hour and an attempted murder every 30 seconds (Simpson, 1985).

In addition to the increasing quantity of violence on "children's" television, it has been argued that there has been a qualitative change in the nature of the violence and the messages conveyed by it (Englehardt, 1986). In the current shows, the machines are often more important than the people and are characterized as being superior to the helpless humans, who require constant protection. The world is never safe because the forces of "evil" are always present waiting to attack the "good." The world faces the threat of total annihilation if the forces of "good" are not constantly vigilant and do not remain strong and superior.

Coupled with the changes in television violence is what may be an even more significant factor: *The nature of the war toys themselves has been changing* more dramatically in recent years than in any time since the invention of the "cap gun" in 1859 (Davis, 1976). Whereas, with the basic cap or water gun, children in the past were required to create their own play around the "shooting" theme, *children can now buy a whole range of war-related toys that are based on the violent television shows they are viewing.* Thus, for most violent children's programs, a line of toys that includes the main characters, scenery, and weapons is marketed, with elaborate packaging describing the attributes of each toy. These "program-based" toys allow and even encourage children to reproduce in play the scripts they have seen on the programs, rather than to invent their own play content.

There has been a change in the relationship between the television and toy industries, resulting in what some critics call the "program-length commercial." This change has become possible to a large extent because of recent rulings by the Federal Communications Commission (FCC), which governs the television industry. In keeping with the general move toward deregulation of the broadcasting industry under the Reagan Administration, the FCC has been gradually eliminating the regulations that used to govern children's television programming. For instance, in 1984 controls were lifted on the number of advertising minutes that were permissible per hour of programming. In 1985 the FCC ruled that product-based programming is legal, which reversed a 1969 ruling banning these programs. The television and toy industries, and even the film industry, have joined forces to take advantage of the new marketing opportunities provided by these FCC changes (Boyer, 1986; Denison, 1985; Englehardt, 1986; Owen, 1986; Raposa, 1986; Segaloff, 1986). For instance, by December of 1985, all of the ten best-selling toys had a television show or had appeared on a "special" program (Denison, 1985). In the fall of 1986, six of the seven animated shows broadcast in New York daily between 3 and 5 o'clock in the afternoon were based on toys (Boyer, 1986). In addition, the success of the movie *Rambo* has led to the rapid introduction of a Rambo doll and a whole line of accompanying toys as well as a Rambo television cartoon series.

The sale of war-related toys, at least in part as a result of these changes, is increasing dramatically. In 1985, sales surpassed $1 billion, up over 400 percent in the last three years (Simpson, 1985). Almost all of the ten best-selling toys for Christmas 1985 were war toys based on television programs. "G.I. Joe," a toy soldier that was taken off the market during the height of the protests against the Vietnam War, has been reintroduced with a whole line of accompanying equipment, as well as a television cartoon, and is among the best sellers. In addition to the increased sale of whole lines of war toys, there has been a dramatic proliferation in the licensing of the characters from the lines to appear on lunch boxes, underwear, toothbrushes, party napkins, and the like. The inundation of violent images children are now experiencing keeps the images ever present in children's minds. Concern about the current situation has led Thomas Radeki, the Founder and Director of the National Coalition on Television Violence, to say that the United States is now raising a "nation of warriors" (Denison, 1985).

Today's children are watching more television than ever before, and at younger ages (Singer, 1983). As early as 9 months of age, children watch television as much as one and a half hours per day. At 3 and 4 years old, children are averaging four hours per day. By elementary-school age, television viewing time steadily increases to an average of four to five hours a day and more on weekends; there are children who spend more time watching television than they do in school.

Adults have long recognized that the quality and content of children's play are influenced by the television they see and the toys they use in their play (Cohen, 1974; Doerkin, 1983; Honig, 1983; Rudolph & Cohen, 1984). But since deregulation, television's influence seems to have increased dramatically. Some educators we spoke with were asking if children's apparently growing desire to play at war is being created and manipulated by the television and toy industries. Because children are now being given toys with which to recreate the ready-made worlds and scripts they have seen on television, the possibility that the content and form of their play is heavily influenced by outside agents is far greater than it ever was in the past.

Whereas concern was previously expressed that television time was taking away from children's play time (Cohen, 1974) and decreasing their interest in play (Winn, 1983), now, even when children have play time, increasingly its content and nature are being dictated by the television and toy industries. This seems to be occurring with children as young as 2 years old. One daycare teacher described significant changes in the dramatic play of the 2-year-olds in her classroom, which she felt occurred when several of the children were introduced at home to one newly marketed violent television cartoon and toy line ("Masters of the Universe"). First these children and then many others went from pretending to shoot pretend dinosaurs and monsters of their own invention, to taking on the role of the "good guy" ("He-man") and pretending to shoot other children, who often became very distressed.

Concerns About the Nuclear Age

There is a fifth and final factor that can help explain the new level of discomfort educators are expressing about children's war play. It has to do with *the issues raised by war play and the current state of the world*. In the words of one school director,

> "In the past it wasn't so critical, but now teachers are asking, 'Is there a relationship between man's aggression and the survival of the world?' And they are asking, 'What is the relationship between how people are and [the nature of] education?'"

Many educators with whom we spoke, who say they at one time found themselves able to accept children's war play on developmental grounds, are now asking whether or not the play has anything to do with real-world violence, and whether or not children can engage in war play without learning militaristic attitudes and values. They are also thinking more now about their own responsibility in relation to the play. The growth in recent years of such professional organizations as Educators for Social Responsibility and Concerned Educators Allied for a Safe Environment attests to the growing awareness among teachers of the potential relationship between their work and world peace. As all of us become more aware of the threat to civilization posed by nuclear war, and as we see the apparent growth in militarism in the world, we find ourselves asking new questions about education and our roles and responsibilities as educators.

CHAPTER 3

Examining the Two Sides of the War Play Debate

As teachers experience the discomfort that often results from the war play dilemma, they are taking a closer look at the two views about war play that are the focus of the current debate. Is there a way to resolve the war play dilemma that addresses both the developmental and sociopolitical points of view, so that accepting one view does not necessitate rejecting the other? We have found it helpful to begin by stepping back and carefully examining the two views and their implications in terms of children's development and learning.

The Developmental View

Underlying the developmental view is the assumption that *play, including war play, is a primary vehicle through which children work on developmental issues.* Is this so and, if so, how and why is this the case?

War Play and Development. Most proponents of the developmental view argue that it is mainly through play that children construct an understanding of concepts and feelings; that play is at the root of children's learning and development (Isaacs, 1937; Piaget, 1951; Smilansky, 1968). Children use play in their own unique ways to make sense of individual experience and to work on the issues of their developmental stage; from their individual experience they choose whatever content for their play they can use to help them work on their developmental issues. As children work on their needs and incorporate new experiences into their play, they encounter information that does not quite fit with their current understanding. This, in turn, causes them to modify their thinking to take into account the newly tried-out information. In this ongoing manner, the content of play gradually evolves and changes as mastery and understanding progress.

17

Thus, the process of play has the potential of supporting children's continuous development, and development is most likely served when the origins and themes of play come from children themselves. When they are in control (Neumann, 1971), they are choosing the content based on their individual needs and experience and on their current level of understanding. Children are the best guides of what they need to work on and when and how. Following from this, developmentalists argue that, because children show a deep interest in war play, it must be an important form of play through which they meet needs and grow (Kostelnik et al., 1986; Wolf, 1984).

Meeting Developmental Needs Through War Play. The potential exists for children to work on numerous developmental issues when they engage in play, including war play. One major task young children face is that of gaining control over their impulses (Kegan, 1982). In war play, children assume the roles of powerful fantasy characters, express aggression in pretend situations, and engage in "pretend fighting," all of which can help them to learn about impulse control as they struggle to stay within acceptable boundaries and receive feedback about their actions from their environment.

Young children are also working on constructing boundaries between fantasy and reality. War play provides children with a special forum for understanding this difference because of the dramatic differences betwen real life and pretending, with regard to the characters and plots involved. Playing out familiar roles in dramatic play is much more tied to children's real experience than pretending to be a fantastic, imaginary character. Also, children can experiment with fantasy characters in a variety of situations and find that there are limits that separate real from imaginary. When a child who is pretending to be a "good guy" pushes another child and claims that he did it because he has "super powers," the responses of the other child and nearby adults help him learn the difference between real and pretend.

Young children are gradually learning to progress beyond egocentrism and to take points of view other than their own (Isaacs, 1937; Kamii & DeVries, 1978, 1980; Piaget & Inhelder, 1969). As children take on contrasting roles (e.g., "good guy" versus "bad guy"), work interdependently with other children in these roles, and see how their actions affect others and others' actions affect themselves, their war play can help them to confront and understand different points of view.

Children are also working on developing a sense of their own competence as separate, autonomous people (Erikson, 1963; Piaget,

1973; White, 1959). This can be exciting but at the same time threatening to the young child. The early years are also a time when children first experience separation from home and separation from their primary caretakers (Balaban, 1985). The sense of power and competence that is experienced in war play—as children pretend to be superheroes with super powers, for instance—can help children feel like strong and separate people who can take care of themselves.

Finally, young children are struggling to understand the things they hear about the world around them, and two of the things they hear about are war and violence in the real world (Carlsson-Paige & Levin, 1985). Children can use their war play as one important vehicle for integrating and making sense out of what they have heard. For example, a child might see soldiers with guns on the television news and bring this image into play in an effort to understand it or to make it less scary.

The Meaning of War Play to Children. Many of the proponents of the developmental view with whom we spoke felt that war play is "just pretend" for most of the children who engage in it—that it is not connected to "real-world" violence in the child's mind. They point to the fact that, while adults may see connections between the play and violence in society, the content and concepts used in children's war play have a different meaning for children than they have for adults (Carlsson-Paige & Levin, 1985). What might the concepts used in war play mean for the young child, from a developmental perspective?

Taking one commonly used concept in children's war play, such as killing and shooting, can be helpful in illustrating the possible meaning of the play for the child. When young children pretend to shoot and kill another child, it generally means quite a different thing to the child than to adults who have the ability to relate the "killing" in the play to actual killing and violence in the real world. Because children do not fully understand time as a continuum, they do not think about death as a permanent and irreversible condition. Because their thinking is egocentric, they can pretend to kill someone else without thinking about it from the point of view of the person killed. And, because of static thinking (i.e., focusing on only one thing at a time), children can pretend to shoot an "enemy" dead at one moment and then interact with that same enemy the next moment. They generally think about what is happening now and not simultaneously about what happened the previous instant. Similarly, for a child who does not establish logical causal connections as adults do, it becomes possible to take on the role of a "bad guy" or "good guy" and "kill" people without thinking about or understanding the meaning or consequences of killing in the real world.

The Appeal of War Play.   It is now possible to see that developmental theory points to a variety of ways in which war play can help young children work on the issues of their stage of development. But this does not necessarily help account for the deep interest many children seem to have in war play. What might account for this "passion"?

First, war play may be a very compelling and deeply satisfying form of play for young children because, perhaps more than most other types of play, it helps them experience power and control. At an age when many of life's experiences can lead to feelings of helplessness and being out of control—for instance, their experiences as they work on the developmental tasks of becoming separate, autonomously functioning individuals—young children are looking for avenues that will help them overcome and progress beyond these feelings.

Second, the content of war play may be especially appealing to young children because of the nature of the thinking that characterizes the early years. Societies have always provided children with much of the content they use in their play; the content for war play that society is currently providing fits neatly with the way children view and interpret their world (Carlsson-Paige & Levin, 1985). They are drawn to the salient perceptual features of things. War and superhero figures provide graphic images for children to use in their play—muscles, ray guns, and explosions. They also tend to think in dichotomous groupings—good or bad, right or wrong, boy or girl—someone cannot be both good and bad simultaneously. War and superhero images embody such black-and-white characteristics.

Third, while the basic "cap gun" of the past appealed to young children because of the power and strength it symbolized, the characteristics of many current war toys are especially well matched to several aspects of young children's thinking and interests. Mechanical toys that can be "transformed" from one thing to another through a sequence of steps (e.g., from an evil robot to a laser bomber plane and back) match children's interests in learning about causality, parts and wholes, and how one thing can be two things. At a time when young children are beginning to work on the transition from static to dynamic thinking—from thinking that is like a series of separate frames of a movie to that which is more like a movie—transformers provide a very appealing cognitive challenge. Similarly, toys that offer the promise of power and strength and that are "like" what children actually see performing dramatic feats on television match children's desire to feel strong while they also provide the concrete and salient images to which children's attention is often drawn.

Finally, it seems that something about war play is especially well matched to the experiences and developmental issues of boys. Our own data and that of others (Paley, 1984) reveal that, while some girls are attracted to war play, it is most often boys who show a compelling interest. This is a controversial issue that currently has many of the adults with whom we spoke perplexed and concerned.

Several arguments can be used to help account for this observed gender difference. It has commonly been attributed to the sex-role stereotyping children experience from the earliest years. According to this argument, boys are encouraged—by their parents, the toys they are given, and the images and role models they see in their environment— to play in more aggressive, less nurturing ways than girls (Singer & Singer, 1981a). From another perspective, both boys and girls are trying to figure out what goes into defining their own gender category (Kohlberg, 1966). At about the age of 18 months, when gender labels are first learned, children begin to look to the world around them, including their families, preschools, and the media, for information about what boys do and what girls do.

Using the environmental-experience argument in conjunction with the cognitive-developmental view can help explain how sex-role stereotyping in the environment might lead to boys' greater interest in war play. If children are seeing and experiencing sex-role stereotyping in their environment, it is these images they will use in constructing their understanding of the roles that accompany the gender labels they have learned. The primarily male superhero figures children see in the media make the distinction between male and female roles clear and simple. They provide boys with some of the most graphic information about male gender roles available in their environment. Many adults question the "macho" attributes these characters embody and feel they are providing boys with undesirable role models. These characters may not be necessary to boys' healthy gender development; at the same time, given that these models do exist, they may be so appealing to boys because they are responding to a genuine need in boys to find clearly defined male models with which to identify.

An additional interesting explanation for why boys have a greater interest in war play than girls comes from theorists who have begun to consider the possibly different courses of development boys and girls go through in the process of achieving gender identification (Chodorow, 1978; Gilligan, 1982). All children must master the experience of separation from home, but, unlike girls, boys must separate from their primary caretakers, primarily still mothers and other females, and also find male gender models with which to identify. This circumstance puts boys under potentially greater stress than girls, who establish their gender identity by identifying with their primary caretaker. Boys must look for alternative models to their nurturing mothers. It also may create in boys a greater feeling of frustration and anger as they try to move away from their mothers and to find avenues for feeling strong and in control without their mothers. Superhero and war figures offer boys the concrete, powerful models that they are seeking, as well as opportunities to express the possible anger and frustration they are feeling.

Play Versus Imitation.   It now seems evident that when we ask whether or not war play can foster children's development, we can answer yes. When we ask how, we can say it is through a complex and active process in which children are using the content of war play to work on the developmental tasks of their stage. When we ask why, we can say that the content of war play is particularly well suited to the thinking of young children and the developmental tasks they face.

At the same time, based on observations of recent changes in some children's play, including war play, some adults who hold the developmental view have begun to ask two additional questions. First, can the quality of children's play affect the degree to which their needs are met in the play (Doerkin, 1983; Rudolph & Cohen, 1984; Schneiderman & Sousa, 1986; Winn, 1983)? Second, if it can, could this be happening now? Applying our current observations about war play, we can ask, When children's play is characterized by conventionality, lack of variety, meager content, and endless repetition and imitation, is optimal development being impeded?

Piaget (1951) makes an important theoretical distinction between play and imitation that can help clarify this recent concern. For Piaget, in play, assimilation predominates over accommodation; whereas, in imitation, accommodation predominates over assimilation. Assimilation is the process by which children take in information from the outside and use it according to their current understanding. Accommodation is the process by which children change their current understanding to take into account information they take in from the outside that does not match their current views. In play, children are in charge of what happens as they change reality to fit their own inner understanding and needs; in imitation, external circumstances take over as children adapt their actions to correspond to the demands and models of the outside world. Piaget admits that, in practice, play does not exist as pure assimilation, that is, by two years of age, some imitation and accommodation are always present in play. These processes serve to provide some of the content for the play and therefore are aids to some of the developmental advance that results. Nonetheless, he argues that, for play to foster optimal development, assimilation, not accommodation, must predominate. According to Piaget,

> Symbolic play is the apogee of children's play. . . . It corresponds to the essential function that play fulfills in the life of the child. Obliged to adapt himself constantly to a social world of elders whose interests and rules remain external to him, and to a physical world which he understands only slightly, the child does not succeed as we adults do in satisfying the affective and even intellectual needs of his personality through these adaptations. It is indispensable to his affective and intellectual equilibrium, therefore, that he have available to him an area of activity whose motivation is not adaptation to reality but, on the contrary, assimilation of reality to the self. . . . Such an area is play, which transforms reality by assimilation to the needs of the self, whereas imitation (when it constitutes an end in itself) is accommodation to external models. [cited in Gruber & Vonèche, 1977, p. 488]

Based on the earlier discussion about how the play process reflects and contributes to development, it does seem possible to say that the degree to which children's needs are met in their war play is affected by the degree to which their activity is play as opposed to imitation, and the degree to which assimilation as opposed to accommodation predominates in the play. As has been described in recent observations of war play, children are using television-based toys to imitate television images and behaviors in their war play, with little variation, elaboration, or evidence that they are making inner meaning of their own from it. Therefore, it does seem possible that thinking and development are not now progressing as optimally through war play as they once did. A sense of mastery and competence is not as likely to be gained, and major developmental issues of the stage such as separation are not as likely to be fully reconciled. There seem to be theoretical grounds for the concerns currently being voiced by adherents of the developmental perspective.

Conclusions.   We can summarize our discussion of the developmental view by concluding that, *while war play can be a vehicle through which children work on meeting their developmental needs,* *playing at war does not necessarily assure that children's needs will be met.* The quality and content of the play will affect the degree to which needs are being met. If the play is primarily imitative of outer experience, which seems to be increasingly the case today, then the interests of development are not optimally served by war play.

The Sociopolitical View

Underlying the sociopolitical view is the assumption that *children learn militaristic political concepts and values through war play.* Most proponents of this view argue that, because children are learning such concepts and attitudes when they engage in war play, the play should not be permitted. Do children learn militaristic political concepts and values through war play? To answer this question we found we first needed to consider more general questions about what the nature of early political concepts might be and whether and how children's political thinking might be developing, both inside and outside of their war play.

Early Political Learning.   Researchers have not directly studied the relationship of children's play to the development of political views. However, drawing from developmental and political socialization theory and research, we can begin to construct a picture of how the content and process of play, including war play, might be used by children to develop the early precursors of adult political thinking.

Most theorists who discuss political socialization argue that political attitudes and ideas have their significant beginnings in the early childhood years (Coles, 1986a, 1986b; Dawson & Prewitt, 1969; Hess & Torney, 1969; Moore, Lare, & Wagner, 1985; Torney-Purta, 1984). According to Easton and Hess,

> Every piece of evidence indicates that the child's political world begins to take shape well before he even enters elementary school and that it undergoes the most rapid change during these years. . . . The truly formative years of the maturing member of a political system would seem to be in the years between three and thirteen. [1962, pp. 237–238]

Political socialization theorists also believe that children's immediate environment plays a crucial role in influencing the content of early political learning (Coles, 1986b; Hess & Torney, 1969). Because the home has been the primary environment of most children in the early years, parents are assumed to play a formative role. For instance, research has shown that older children's political attitudes tend to reflect those of their parents more than they do those of other environmental influences (Torney-Purta, 1984). The additional finding that political attitudes change the most up to about the age of 13 and are less subject to change thereafter has led to the argument that special attention should be paid to political education in the early years, including that in the school (Torney-Purta, 1984).

What is the nature of early political concepts? What might the process through which they are developed be, and what might the role of war play be in that process? What are the factors that might influence the nature of the ideas that develop? Building onto the earlier discussion of the developmental view, it is possible to begin to answer these questions.

Constructing Early Political Concepts. Adults have political concepts about such things as nations and homeland, governments, laws governing behavior in society, global conflict, and interdependence among people. Based on our earlier discussion, it is important to keep in mind that children's early political concepts about these things will be quite different from those of adults, because of the differences that characterize the thinking of children and adults (Piaget & Weil, 1951). It is also important in this discussion to realize that there is not necessarily a one-to-one correspondence between the content of children's war play and the outside world; moreover, the meaning of the content of war play to children may not match the meaning ascribed to the content by adults.

Political concepts are constructed gradually as individuals pass through a series of predictable developmental stages and construct individual and unique meaning from experience. Young children, because of their developmental level, begin to develop political concepts from concrete experience in all aspects of their lives, and these concepts will not necessarily be logical or coherent from the adult point of view (Kamii & Devries, 1978, 1980). Concepts such as democracy and government by law may have their origins, at least in part, in children's early experiences with family and classroom decision making (Wyner, 1978) and the rules by which they learn to govern their interactions with others (Piaget, 1965). These early concepts will begin to form before children have much understanding of governments and the electoral and law-making processes. Children's first understanding of the concepts of world peace and international relations will be influenced by early experiences in resolving conflicts and establishing reciprocity with others in their immediate environment (Bruner, 1960; Carlsson-Paige & Levin, 1985), rather than from significant awareness of real conflicts among nations. Concepts about friends and enemies at the global level will grow out of such things as children's social experiences with peers, their exposure to similarities and differences among people, and how this exposure is treated by the adults around them. These concepts will not be a reflection of a more abstract understanding of nationalities and ethnic groups.

As children experience or hear about the political aspects of the world at large, they gradually incorporate this information into their early political concepts by trying to relate what they are hearing to the meaning they have previously constructed. Thus, a child's early concept of "enemy," which is based in part on experiences of cooperation and conflict with other children, may come to include specific names and labels (e.g., Russians and Germans), as these labels are heard. But only gradually will any of these labels become fully defined categories that resemble adult concepts.

The fact that children's early political views can look quite different to observers from those of adults has often led to children's political views going unrecognized as being such by researchers. For instance, Robert Coles (1986b) describes how it took him many years to recognize the fact that much of what young children were telling him in interviews about their views of the world revealed a great deal of political understanding about how society and relationships among different groups of people worked. At the same time, there are many adults who have looked at children's war play and attributed a whole range of political concepts of a militaristic nature to the play, when these concepts were perhaps not present. In both cases, a better understanding of the nature of early political concepts and how they might be reflected in war play could assist all adults in their work with children.

Political Learning and War Play. Because play is a primary vehicle through which young children make sense of what they experience and construct new ideas, it follows that play is an important avenue for constructing early political concepts. Adults need to understand war play in the child's terms in order to understand the nature of the political concepts that children might be forming in the play and the relationship these concepts have to the real world for the child. For instance, what such things as "killing" or being the "good guy" or "bad guy" mean to any given child and how they are used in play will be unique and changing, and their meaning for the child will only gradually begin to approximate adult meaning. The same is true for the language children bring to their war play: Words such as "lasers," "nuclear bombs," "the Russians," and "the world" have different meaning to children than to adults.

In most play, especially if others are involved and regardless of its specific content, some political learning can be involved. For instance, in "house" play, lessons are learned about conflict and conflict resolution as two children argue over wanting the role of "father" and reach a compromise solution. However, war play is a form of play that has the potential for exerting an especially powerful influence on the political ideas children construct. Its very nature and content are permeated with issues of power and conflict, right and wrong, good and evil, safety and danger, and friends and enemies—all of which are basic components of political concepts. For instance, as children play out power relationships in their war play, what they learn about power is part of the foundation of later adult understanding of power relations among people, groups of people, and nations. Children can construct meaning about friends and enemies as they pretend that an alien space creature attacks their building in the block corner. They are learning about power and subservience as a child role-playing "He-man" scares other children as he chases them into a corner. Similarly, rule-governed behavior is better understood as a group of children agree to play a superhero chase game by all adhering to the same set of rules.

As with the development of early concepts outside of play, the formation of concepts through play, including political concepts, is an ongoing and interactive process whereby a child gets information from the world, brings it into play, constructs understanding of it in play, and in turn brings this new meaning back to the world, to be used to interpret further experience. It is in this fashion that children gradually connect the political concepts they construct in play, which in part originated in the real world, to their growing knowledge of the real world. Therefore, especially because fantasy and reality can be meshed in the young child's mind, the political concepts constructed in "fantasy" war play have the potential for influencing how real-world experience is interpreted.

For example, a child may see G.I. Joe shooting his enemy on television and incorporate this image into play, pretending to shoot a child who is the "bad guy" with a stick. Through this play the child will be actively constructing meaning about such things as shooting, "bad guys," conflict, and the role of violence. Some of the meaning of the shooting action in the play will have come from the child's experience prior to seeing G.I. Joe on television, while some will be taken from the shooting image that was seen on television. Then, when this child hears on television news that the United States is "shooting" at Libya, she will interpret it in terms of everything she knows about shooting, enemies, and conflict, some of which has been constructed in her play. Through this ongoing and interactive process, whereby new experience is connected to prior concepts through play, children's political concepts gradually develop.

Sources of the Political Content of War Play. Much of the content in children's war play, including the political content (e.g., who the enemies are, the reasons for using weapons, or how problems among players are resolved), is influenced by social agents outside of the child—the family, the school, mass media, and peer groups. The values and goals that a society has for its children will affect the nature of the political content it provides to children for play.

First, as children are exposed to the objects, events, and values of the world around them, they take pieces of what they experience and hear to use in their play. If they are exposed to or hear about real or fictionalized violence (which are not always differentiated by the child), then this is likely to affect the content of their war play. During World War II, British children used experiences of the German bombing of Britain in their war play (Freud & Burlingham, 1943). In Northern Ireland, Catholic children have been reported to use British soldiers as enemies in their play (Lyons, 1971). American teachers have recently observed that Russians as enemies, nuclear bombs as weapons, and radiation as a destructive force have become part of the content of many children's war play (Carlsson-Paige & Levin, 1985).

Second, the toys for war play provided by a society to its children, as well as how a society treats children's efforts to use the toys, will affect the content of war play. The toys in a given society can even be seen as a reflection of that society's dominant social and political values at a particular time in history. For example, currently, all children's war toys are banned in Sweden (Swedish Information Service, 1980). Such a ban, which began voluntarily and is now being implemented by the government, can be seen as a reflection of Sweden's nonmilitaristic posture in the world and its policymakers' efforts to develop policies that help to socialize children into this political philosophy. There are voluntary curbs on the sale of war toys in West Germany, as well. There is an obvious contrast between these policies and current practices in the United States. It may not be a coincidence that the recent rapid increase in the sale of war-related toys in the

United States comes at a time when government policy is directed toward large increases in defense spending. One can be led to question whether or not there is a relationship between the current climate toward defense and the toys children are offered with which to create the content of their play (Engelhardt, 1986).

Third, the adult role models that a society provides to its children to use in their play and the values that accompany those models can affect the political content and political views that develop in war play. Researchers argue that there is a relationship between the content and form of children's play and the larger society in which it takes place. According to Sutton-Smith and Roberts (1981), cross-cultural research has helped to show how various forms of play both reflect a culture and prepare children for membership in that culture. There is also some relationship between roles practiced in childhood play and adult roles later assumed (Sutton-Smith & Roberts, 1981). Following from this, we might ask what it means when one set of roles and the attitudes and concepts associated with those roles become emphasized by a society in its children's play. More specifically, what does it mean when a society seems to be channeling its boys so extensively into war play? Is such a society narrowing the potential range of adult role options that are available for its children and thereby channeling its children into certain adult choices and attitudes?

Finally, the media are becoming an increasingly important source of the content, political and otherwise, of children's play, including war play. While in the past researchers have focused primarily on the influences of television news programs on children's knowledge and attitudes (Doerkin, 1983), or on the effects of television viewing on children's aggression and play (Honig, 1983; Singer & Singer, 1981b, 1984), the ways in which television may be affecting the development of children's political concepts has not been carefully studied. However, as children spend more and more time watching television, especially programs of a militaristic and violent nature, developmental theory would lead to the prediction that the themes they see will affect the content of their play.

There is obvious political content in the television programs that are currently being produced for children. For example, most current animated programs contain political content that many critics say is of a militaristic nature (Engelhardt, 1986; Schneiderman & Sousa, 1986; Simpson, 1985). There are always good guys against bad guys, and children are encouraged to identify with the good guys, who always win. Humans are depicted as weak and powerless unless they have machines and an arsenal of weapons to protect them. The good guys

CASTLE GRAYSKULL
RAMBO
GIA JOE MOUNTAIN
SNAKE MOUNTAIN
SNOUT SPOUT BATTLE RAM
WHUMANBUZZ-OFF
INHUMANOIDS
MAS KOIDS PANTHOR
WIND-RAIDER SPYDOR BLASTERHAWK
STRATO BATTLECAT EEL
LIFE SIZT THUNDERCATS SWORD
HURRICANE HORDAC
THE JOKER MOBILE ROBOT LOVE ANDREW

TRI-KLOPS
BEAST-MAN
EVIL-LYN
PRINCE ADAM
MER-MAN
HANDCFFS
THUNDR THE CATS

LOVE Andrew

face the constant threat of complete annihilation unless they remain stronger and better armed than the bad guys (enemies), who are often depicted as speaking in unfamiliar, foreign-sounding and distorted voices and are sometimes faceless and dehumanized. Fighting is glamorized partly because the physical, human pain that results from fighting is almost never depicted. To feel powerful and strong is equated with a sense of well being. Disagreements are always terminated by violence; dialogues between "good" and "bad" sides are never depicted, and attempts to see another's point of view are not portrayed. Women are generally depicted in roles that are subservient to men, and on occasion they are treated in ways that some critics label as misogynistic (Schneiderman & Sousa, 1986). The observation that much of this content can teach children to behave in dehumanized, aggressive, and warlike ways and to value physical strength, power, and violence has led many critics to argue that television is providing children with distinctly militaristic content and values for their play.

In summary, we can now say that young children's political thinking can look quite different and have quite different meaning from the political concepts of adults. When we ask how early political concepts might be constructed, we can say that children receive political content from a variety of sources in their environment. Because play is a primary vehicle for making sense out of experience, children use what they hear in their play, including war play, as a means of gradually constructing political concepts. They do this at their own developmental level and in ways that are unique to each individual. Finally, when we ask what the nature of the political concepts children are learning might be, we can say that what children learn depends on the content that they are getting from society and the individual meaning that they are making through their own play.

Militaristic Political Concepts and War Play.   We now need to ask whether or not the political concepts children are learning as they engage in war play are necessarily of a militaristic nature and, if so, what the long-term impact on political thinking might be. These are complex questions which researchers have not directly asked. To answer them fully would require longitudinal research tracing the development of political and militaristic ideas, beginning with a close look at the nature and content of play in the early years. However, based on what *is* known, we can begin to make conjectures about possible answers to these questions.

It seems essential to this discussion to distinguish between children learning general political concepts about such things as war, weapons, and conflict and children developing militaristic political concepts about these things. When children engage in any dramatic play, they are constructing some kind of understanding about the content of that play. While some adults might argue that all war play is teaching content of a militaristic nature, we feel that there is a difference between developing concepts about war, conflict, and violence and developing attitudes of militarism. What distinguishes the two?

In the first place, the nature and quality of the play are of crucial importance. We must assess whether it is primarily "play," with assimilation predominating and the child in control of the content, or whether it is mainly "imitation," with accommodation predominating and the content coming primarily from the outside world. When assimilation is dominant and children are creating their own war play out of a rich experience base, they are the active agents in constructing their own political knowledge. When they select bits and pieces from experience and incorporate them into their dynamic play, they are choosing the information that is most relevant to their needs and political understanding at that moment. When their roles and actions are fluid and changing, their political knowledge is more likely to be expanding, deepening, and advancing. Under such conditions, play is fulfilling its function as a primary vehicle through which children construct concepts and the basic foundation for later political understanding is solidly formed in developmentally appropriate ways. As a result, children are likely to bring the political concepts constructed in their play, which are of their own making, back to their interpretations of and actions in the real world, in a meaningful way.

Children can engage in this rich assimilative play process and learn political concepts that establish the foundations for understanding peace and how to work toward it, or, by the same means, they can establish the foundations of militarism and violence. We would argue, however, that without the primacy of assimilation in war play, the political ideas children use in their play are more likely to be imitations of what they have seen rather than understanding of their own construction. In such a situation, children are likely to be mimicking the militaristic ideas they have been exposed to, without constructing a foundation for their own political ideas and understanding. Therefore, one important gauge for deciding the degree to which war play is teaching militarism will be the amount of originality and elaboration it contains, as opposed to imitation and repetition.

When children are involved in a rich, assimilative war play process, they are certainly learning about war, conflict, and violence. But, whether or not this learning is contributing to militaristic attitudes will depend on a second factor, namely, the total context in which the play occurs. The contextual information provided to children has the potential to create the disequilibrium in thinking that can ultimately help children expand the militaristic concepts they have formed. For example, this can occur when children are encouraged to think of a variety of ways to approach and solve problems, to negotiate disputes, to see the consequences of their actions, and to understand and value the point of view of others (Carlsson-Paige & Levin, 1985; Kohlberg, 1969). The context can serve to lessen the impact of the militaristic content that children bring to their war play from society. It can also help expand the repertoire of nonmilitaristic political ideas they will use in the play. Therefore, the total culture that surrounds a child (i.e., parents, teachers, mass media, peers) will affect the role war play will have in the development of a child's militaristic attitudes.

The context in which children's play occurs is important in another way. It is important to ask how children bring the militaristic content of their war play into nonplay situations. For example, if a child is using the kind of violence seen on television in real, nonplay interactions with other children, then militarism might be affecting the concept the child is forming about how interpersonal relationships are conducted outside of fantasy play.

Thus, a second useful gauge for deciding whether or not war play is contributing to militaristic attitudes is to consider the total context in which the play occurs, the degree to which the child carries militaristic ideas from play into that context, and the extent to which that context challenges and expands political thinking.

Finally, as we look at war play and conclude that the concepts being learned in the play can be of a militaristic nature, we must consider what the potential long-term impact might be. There are many factors that can affect how early political attitudes and concepts change as more mature thinking develops (Dawson & Prewitt, 1969; Gibbs & Schnell, 1985; Kohlberg, 1969). However, because development is a continuous process and because the understanding of a political concept that a child begins to construct is used to make sense of new information that is encountered in an ongoing manner, we have to assume that what happens in childhood has the potential for having a central influence on later political thinking. Therefore, we need to take the question of whether children are learning militaristic political concepts through their war play seriously, if we are to think about how as educators we hope to educate children to work toward finding ways of living peacefully in the world.

Militaristic Learning and Current Concerns About War Play. How can the previous discussion about the political content and learning in war play help us understand the observations many educators and parents have made about recent changes in play?

Children use their play as a vehicle for building knowledge out of what they have experienced; thus, as they are exposed to an increasing amount of violence on television, as is the case today, violence will be reflected in the content of their play. Similarly, increasing amounts of their play time, which continues to be reduced for many children because of the increasing amount of time spent viewing television, will be used trying to construct an understanding of the violence they have seen.

At the same time, for play to fulfill its optimal role in development, it should be primarily assimilative and stem from the child's needs. This process is increasingly hampered because (1) children are getting a greater proportion of the content for their play from passively watching television of a violent nature and (2) they are given ready-made toys with which to re-create the violent scripts in their play. As a result, they will be more likely to imitate and "pseudo-accommodate" what they have seen rather than to make the play their own. In such a situation, children are less likely to develop meaning for themselves that can grow and change over time; to construct their own cognitive categories for use as a basis for organizing understanding; to work out an understanding of causality for themselves; to decide for themselves what is real and what is not real; or to feel that they are in full control of what happens in their play (Isaacs, 1937; Piaget, 1951).

When the quality of children's play is distorted in these ways and when children are exposed to increasing amounts of militarism and violence, then the concepts they form that mirror what they have seen are more likely to be militaristic. The aggressiveness that they exhibit thus may be more a reflection of what they are imitating than an indication of their own needs to work out aggressive feelings or experience a sense of power. When this happens, the loss of connection between children's needs and their behaviors can lead to many of the changes adults are reporting about current war play: more aggressive and hard-to-manage behavior in the classroom because children are not adequately working out their own developmental needs; more obsessive involvement in war play because imitative play is less effective in helping children to construct meaning; and more militaristic behavior in and out of war play because the concepts learned in war play are often "mirrors" of outside influences. While many parents and teachers we talked with tended to criticize one another for causing the increased aggression and violence in children's play, neither group is really to blame.

We feel that a strong case can be made for concluding that recent changes in society, especially changes in the media and toy industries (which may reflect the broader political climate), are leading to many of the concerns about war play that are currently causing the war play dilemma to be felt with such intensity by so many adults. The massive bombardment of violent and combative images that children are now experiencing from television, coupled with the availability of toys that lead children to re-create these images, is probably having a major impact on the content and quality of children's war play and their developing political ideas.

Conclusion: War Play Today and the Two Views

We can now say that there are possible theoretical explanations for the concerns many adults are currently expressing about war play. From the developmental viewpoint, such play may not be serving children's needs to the degree that it once did. From the sociopolitical viewpoint, the play may be becoming more militaristic. Each of these views has the potential for contributing to the understanding of the other: Teachers cannot optimally affect the development of children's political ideas without considering the developmental perspective, and, if we only address developmental issues, we are not fully appreciating the political influences on children's lives today.

Where does this leave us in deciding how to respond to war play? We will need an approach for working with children that incorporates both the developmental and sociopolitical points of view, in order to address fully children's and adults' needs in these times.

CHAPTER 4

A Closer Look at War Play: Two Examples

Careful observation of children's war play can help adults assess the degree to which children's play tends toward being more symbolic or imitative. Observations can also tell us a great deal about how children are using the play to work out developmental issues as well as the kinds of sociopolitical learning that might be occurring.

In the following two play sequences, 4-year-old boys were observed as they each engaged in dramatic play involving themes of power and destruction.

Example 1: Jackson

The subject of the first sequence, Jackson, does not watch violent cartoon programs or have the toys that accompany these programs. He engaged in the following play sequence after visiting a museum where he viewed a cartoon in which a tyrannosaurus rex terrorized other dinosaurs and then killed and ate a pterodactyl in a violent and bloody scene. That evening, playing at home, Jackson went and got out his own collection of dinosaurs.

Jackson picks up his toy tyrannosaurus and crashes it into other dinosaurs, knocking them down and saying, "I'm smashing your bones. I got your eyes. I'm gonna grind you up . . . eat you up." He keeps hitting the dinosaurs with the tyrannosaurus over and over again with ferocity. Jackson hands a brontosaurus to his grandmother and tells her, "Say, 'Oh, please don't kill me. I don't wanna die' when the tyrannosaurus comes." The grandmother does this, but Jackson's tyrannosaurus smashes her dinosaur to the ground as he says, "You're dead."

Jackson next picks up two dinosaurs and has one say to the other, "Quick, put your head in my mouth. I won't hurt you.

I'm going to help you." The "helping" dinosaur carries the "victim" dinosaur in its mouth to a hiding place behind the couch as Jackson says, "Stay here. You're safe." One by one Jackson puts each of the dinosaurs' heads into the mouth of the "helper" and deposits them behind the couch. Then, this helping dinosaur goes and smashes into the tyrannosaurus, saying, "You're dead." Jackson grabs a stick from his toy drum set and hits the tyrannosaurus. "Now the other dinosaurs will be safe," he says. He carries the tyrannosaurus to another room and brings all the other dinosaurs out from behind the couch while singing, "Yeah, yeah, the tyrannosaurus is dead" (to the tune of "Ding, Dong, The Witch Is Dead" from *The Wizard of Oz*). Jackson says, "Now, the whole family is safe." He then goes to get the tyrannosaurus, saying, "You're going to have to live in a cage." He builds an elaborate cage for the tyrannosaurus and says, "He used to be in the family, but he's so bad they kicked him out."

Jackson's play grows out of his exposure to the violent cartoon and involves the themes of power and mastery, good and bad, and violence. As we look at this play scenario, we can see how it changes from beginning to end. In the beginning Jackson uses only information he brings in from the cartoon; then he begins to take information he has learned from other experience and apply it to this situation (e.g., he incorporates his experience with his family and with a book he was read in which small animals hide in the mouth of a lion). It begins as repetitive violence with a single focus, becomes violence within a story context, and ends as violence overcome and restrained (i.e., tyrannosaurus in a cage). At first, the world is a threatening and hostile place; by the end it becomes a place where the family of dinosaurs can live in peace and safety. In addition, the play begins with Jackson taking the point of view and assuming the power of the mighty tyrannosaurus. He gradually incorporates the point of view of the victim ("Oh, please don't kill me!") and finally stands back as the orchestrator of a "small world" of characters where power shifts to his family of "good" dinosaurs.

As we look at Jackson's play we can see that it seems to progress through a series of phases. In the first phase, Jackson primarily imitates what he has seen; he hits his toy dinosaurs with the tyrannosaurus rex over and over again. This is a fairly rigid phase in which he is using something new that he has experienced (the violent cartoon scene) in the form in which he has seen it. In the next phase, Jackson begins to elaborate the new idea, to introduce a variation on the cartoon script, by bringing in his grandmother and her role. Next, Jackson enters a third phase in which he really begins to invent a new story: He creates new roles (e.g., the helping dinosaur); uses new props (e.g., the couch, the other room); and brings his own developmental concerns into the play, especially separation (feelings of being included in or excluded from the family) and mastery (overcoming fear from having seen the scary cartoon).

Jackson is feeling comfortable enough to experiment freely with major variations on the original idea. He is able to use the play to work on his own developmental concerns and to construct his own understanding of concepts. For example, he tries out one way of eliminating the threat of the tyrannosaurus (by killing it) and then experiments with another less violent means (by building a cage). As he does this, Jackson's understanding of violence and how to resolve conflicts expands a little. He also learns about cooperation as he devises ways that the dinosaurs can help each other. This is the phase in which the active invention of new ideas occurs. It is the phase of play in which Jackson takes full control, making his own meaning out of a new experience. Toward the end of the play scenario, Jackson reaches a final phase in which he finds a resolution to the story; he creates a world free of the threat of tyrannosaurus rex and, along with this, experiences a sense of his own empowerment.

Example 2: Jay

The second play sequence was observed during a typical afternoon in which a 4-year-old boy, Jay, watched some television cartoons and then played with his action figures and toy weapons.

> Jay grabs a small toy knife and sticks it many times into an action figure from "Masters of the Universe." He says, "You're dead, you're dead." He throws the doll away, saying, "I got you. You're crushed. . . . You're dead." He pulls out another figure and repeats the sticking action with the knife. Jay gets up and goes to the kitchen. A few minutes later he returns and stomps on the two "dead" figures, then picks up a transforming action toy (in its "tank" form). He carefully changes it into the robot form and attaches a gun to one hand and a big fist to the other. He runs over to the two "dead" characters and goes "Pow, pow. Now you're really dead. I killed you. I'm He-

Man!" He goes over to several other action figures (fierce-looking robot characters with bulging muscles) and picks up each one, examining it carefully. Holding the He-Man figure he says, "Get ready . . . it's the bad guys. The evil Decepticons! It's really gonna be bad. Get ready. Get ready." He picks up a toy machine gun and rapidly repeats, "Pow, pow, pow!" as he shoots at his bad-guy action figures that are lying on the floor. He puts the gun down and returns to the kitchen to ask when it's his birthday. He says he wants to get "M.U.S.C.L.E. Invaders."

As we look at Jay's play, we can see the themes of good guys against bad guys, power, and violence. He is identifying with the good guys and is being strong and powerful as he repeatedly "kills" the bad guys. He seems to be imitating aspects of what he has seen on television, but, unlike Jackson's play, Jay's play does not seem to change significantly from beginning to end.

Jay's action figures serve as props to represent good and bad, but he doesn't develop their characters beyond this or bring in any other props to use along with them. He uses the themes of good versus bad and violence as separate from a story or context of his own making. He does not bring in information he has learned from other experiences to develop and change the characters and themes.

Jay's play seems to involve several self-contained scenarios rather than to progress through phases. He plays out the same themes, using different toys, in a repetitive way. Throughout this entire play episode, Jay seems to remain in the more imitative phase which we observed as Jackson's first phase of play. He doesn't progress to a phase in which he is actively inventing his own meaning out of the images he has been given—where he takes what he has seen and changes it into something of his own making. Because of this, Jay's understanding of violence and conflict resolution does not expand, through his play, beyond the images he has seen. In addition, he is not able to use the play to work on developmental issues that are important to him; his deepest issues do not seem to connect with what he is doing as he plays. Jay never reaches a point where he is comfortable enough to take control of the play in a way that provides him with a sense of empowerment or feeling of resolution.

The contrast between Jackson's and Jay's play is striking. If their play is representative of their play in general, then the implications for the overall development of each child are significant. Jackson plays in a way that child development and play theory have long described as vital to healthy development. Jay is playing in a way that typifies many of the descriptions teachers and parents have given us as they express their concerns about how children's play might be changing in the current social context.

CHAPTER 5

Deciding on an Approach to War Play: Considering the Options

As we questioned teachers about how they dealt with war play in their classrooms, their responses could, for the most part, be grouped into four possible approaches:

Option 1: Ban war play
Option 2: Take a laissez-faire approach to war play
Option 3: Allow war play, with predetermined limits
Option 4: Actively facilitate war play

Teachers perform roles as agents of society in the socialization process of children (Wilson, 1975). They also have a role in fostering children's development (Elkind, 1976). With respect to war play, these two roles generally fall into one or the other side of the war play debate and, as with the debate, teachers often find it difficult to address both of these roles simultaneously. Thus, when a teacher chooses an approach to war play, she or he seems to be choosing to emphasize one or the other of these two crucial roles.

Most of the teachers we questioned banned war play. These teachers tended to see the play more in terms of its significance in the political socialization process and their role and responsibility as agents of society. There were also some teachers who did allow war play in some form. They tended to see the play more in terms of its relationship to child development and their role and responsibility in supporting that development through war play. It seemed that, in choosing an approach to war play, teachers were implicitly or explicitly making a choice as to which of their roles and responsibilities as educators they wanted to emphasize in relation to the play. At the same time, no matter what approach they chose or what priorities they set around their responsibilities for responding to war play, many

43

teachers seemed aware that, by choosing the approach they did, they
were not adequately addressing the other side of the debate. They
realized that they were not adequately resolving the war play dilemma
as it exists today.

When teachers ban war play, thereby addressing the sociopolitical
side of the war play debate, are they actually fulfilling their roles and
responsibilities as agents of socialization? When teachers address the
developmental side of the debate and allow war play, are they actually
serving to foster children's development? And, as with the war play
dilemma, when they opt to emphasize one role over the other by
allowing or banning the play, what about their responsibility to
perform the other role?

Let us examine the four options in terms of how well they fulfill
teachers' responsibilities to foster children's development and to serve
as social agents who foster nonmilitaristic political concepts and attitudes in children.

Option 1: Ban War Play

> "We have a strictly enforced 'no guns in school' rule. If a child
> persists after the rule is explained ('guns hurt people—we don't
> even want to pretend to hurt people'), the child is put in time-
> out. . . . And unfortunately, some children seem to be obsessed
> with it and often end up in time out."

With the banning approach, teachers tell children they are not
allowed to engage in any kind of war and weapons play, sometimes
giving an explanation and sometimes not. A lot of teachers choose this
option because, in keeping with the sociopolitical view, they feel that
allowing the play leads to the development of militaristic attitudes.
When they ban, they do not have to experience the discomfort that
arises when the play conflicts with their own desire to teach nonviolence. In fact, teachers often feel that by banning the play they are
actually teaching nonviolence, as they take a stand that violence in all
forms is bad (Schneiderman & Sousa, 1986). Finally, the banning
approach is also attractive to teachers because it precludes the disci-
pline problems that often result from war play.

Does the banning option fulfill teachers' responsibility to help
children meet their developmental needs through play? If war play is
particularly well suited to meeting certain of children's developmental
needs, and if children need the play in order to work out an understanding of the war-related images and content they have been exposed
to, then obviously teachers who ban the play are depriving children of

an important vehicle for meeting their needs (Kostelnik et al., 1986; Wolf, 1984). It becomes especially important in these times, when children's exposure to violence is on the rise and their need to work through what they have seen through play increases, to consider the effects of banning the play on children.

In addition, there are other risks associated with banning war play that relate to children's overall development. For instance, as in the preceding quote, children are told that war play is wrong from the adult's point of view (i.e., "guns hurt people—we don't even want to pretend to hurt people"). Such an approach not only denies children the opportunity to work out their developmental needs in war play but runs the risk of producing guilt in children when they are made to feel that their attempts to meet their developmental needs through play are bad. Even in the best of situations, where children are gently told that school is not a place for war play, children get the message that at least one of their passionate interests has nothing to do with school, and teachers miss out on one important channel for reaching at least some children.

Does banning war play adequately address the role of the teacher in fostering children's political socialization? While the banning approach often allows teachers to feel that they are teaching nonviolence, the end effect of such an approach is that children are left to play at war whenever they can find the opportunity, using the images they have been handed from the world around them. By choosing not to influence the political concepts that children are constructing in their play, teachers are, in effect, giving up one central avenue they have for affecting the political socialization process. Perhaps most important, by interpreting war play completely from their own adult political perspective, they are ignoring what the war play means to children and how children develop political concepts.

In sum, while this approach does a good job of addressing the needs of teachers, it does not adequately take into account the teacher's responsibility to children. A banning approach can eliminate problems and controversy from the classroom, but it leaves too much of children's development—the meeting of their needs and the growth of their political understanding—to social forces outside of the classroom.

Option 2: Take a Laissez-faire Approach to War Play

"The kids in my classroom love war play. I think they need to be able to play in their own way without my interference, so I don't usually get involved unless someone is getting hurt."

With this approach in its pure form, teachers openly allow children to play in whatever ways they choose. In its more diluted form, teachers, perhaps feeling more ambivalent and somewhat trapped by the war play dilemma, turn their backs and allow the play, without directly condoning it. This option appeals to many teachers who basically want to support children's needs and who see that children have a genuine interest in war play. It can be a positive thing for children to feel that their needs and the forms of play that they enjoy are accepted by the teacher.

But does the laissez-faire approach actually meet children's developmental needs and fulfill a teacher's responsibility in helping to meet them? The approach does create the potential for children to work on their developmental needs through war play, but, because it does not involve a role for the teacher, it leaves to chance whether or not these needs are met. While in other forms of dramatic play teachers often take on a more active role in facilitating and helping to elaborate play (such as by suggesting a new role or prop), with the laissez-faire approach to war play, children are left to develop the play to the extent that they can do this on their own. By choosing not to influence the play, teachers are relinquishing an important area that they could affect. In addition, the teacher's nonparticipation leaves the question of safety up to the children. If children do not feel a sense of safety in their play, this can affect the quality of their play and the extent to which they are able to work on important issues through play. While children vary considerably in their ability to keep their play safe for themselves, it is rarely the case that all children will be able to feel secure in war play if the teacher is not providing any external controls.

Can the laissez-faire approach fulfill a teacher's responsibility in fostering political socialization? Because the teacher is not involved in children's war play in any significant way with this approach, children are left to develop in play the images that they have received from outside agents in a manner identical to that which occurs when the banning approach is adopted. However, unlike the banning approach, with the laissez-faire approach, teachers generally do not confuse their own political views with children's war play.

In sum, this option does not address children's needs or teachers' responsibilities adequately. At a time when the quality of children's play is called into question, and when children seem to need help in developing their war play and the political concepts it involves, it seems doubtful that a teacher who adopts the laissez-faire approach is making the best choice.

Option 3: Allow War Play, with Specific Limits

"I allow the play to go on outside as long as no one gets hurt. The rule is usually that it's okay outdoors if all parties are willing participants and if it's done with pretend, not toy guns."

With this approach, as with the laissez-faire approach, teachers allow war play but in this case they place one or more clearly spelled-out limits on it. They may specify the space where the play can occur, such as only on the playground or in the block area. They may place limits on the times during the day when the play can occur, such as only at the beginning of the day or at recess. Limits may be placed on the materials allowed for the play, such as no toy guns, fingers only; only child-made weapons; no action figures. Or, teachers may establish rules guiding the social interactions in the play; for example, children must mutually agree to engage in the play or agree on what roles they will assume, and refrain from actual physical contact.

This option is attractive to many teachers because, as with the laissez-faire approach, children do have the opportunity to use war play to meet their needs. Compared to the laissez-faire approach, because of the clearly spelled-out limits, it is more likely to provide an environment where children are helped to stay in control and feel safe as they play. At the same time, teachers feel they are more in control of what happens because they are taking a position on some of the boundaries of the play, and in some cases even stating clear positions on the degree of violence that occurs. In a sense, this is a middle-of-the-road approach that does begin to address both developmental and sociopolitical issues.

But how adequately does this option fulfill the teacher's responsibilities in both areas? In terms of developmental issues, with this approach, as with the laissez-faire approach, no attention is given to the teacher's role in facilitating the play process. Therefore, while the play is allowed to occur in school, the degree to which children meet their developmental needs through play is still left up to them. However, while this approach does focus on limiting and containing children's war play—something the laissez-faire approach does not do—because the limits are predetermined and imposed on children by the teacher, they are set independently of what individual children's needs are or what the quality of the play might require.

In terms of sociopolitical issues, if a teacher limits the play in certain ways but does not become actively involved in it, then the political and social concepts that a child is working out are once again left to other societal forces. There is no meaningful connection between the ideas children are working to understand through play and the teacher's values and goals. Children may know that their teacher disapproves of guns because toy guns are not allowed in their war play, but how does this fit with the many things they have heard about guns, war, and politics outside the classroom, things that have become part of their play?

We feel that this is not an adequate approach because it restricts the teacher's role in terms of both the facilitation of children's play and the development of their political concepts. These limitations make this option insufficient as a choice for teachers.

Option 4: Actively Facilitate War Play

"It has taken me a long time to accept children's need to engage in war play and to make it a part of my classroom curriculum. I've had to get past a lot of obstacles in my own thinking. But this year I have been allowing the play with some limits. And I've become involved in the play myself, observing children and intervening in a lot of different ways."

With this option, teachers allow children to engage in war and weapons play; however, teachers become actively involved in facilitating the play in order to help children use the play in ways that further their development and their political knowledge.

Teachers try to get a picture of how individual children are using their play to work out feelings and ideas, and what social and political concepts they are constructing in play. As with other forms of dramatic play (e.g., house play), teachers then routinely intervene by helping children expand and elaborate their play; they may suggest new roles, offer new materials, temporarily assume a role in play themselves, and use and expand developing concepts. Teachers do this in order to help children use their play in ways that foster optimal conceptual and social growth, creativity, and problem-solving ability (Smilansky, 1968, 1971). By intervening in order to help the children expand and elaborate their war play, teachers are thereby affecting the quality of the play in terms of both developmental and political issues.

How can such an approach to war play meet a teacher's responsibilities to children in these times? The disadvantages in choosing it are probably clear to most teachers. It is a difficult approach to accept. It brings within the teacher's responsibility a cluster of images and behaviors that many teachers would prefer to banish permanently from their classrooms. It places extra demands on the teacher's ability to maintain a safe environment for children and to influence children's developing political concepts.

There are, however, two major reasons why this option best meets a teacher's responsibility to children. First, when children are permitted to engage in war play in the classroom with the teacher playing an active role, they have the optimal opportunity to work on their developmental issues through play and the teacher has the opportunity to influence the quality of play. The teacher is there, insuring that the war play is serving to foster children's optimal development. The teacher is helping the children to gain control over their impulses, to take points of view other than their own, to distinguish between fantasy and reality, to work out their own understanding about what they have heard about the world around them, and to experience a sense of their own power and mastery through play.

The second major reason is that this option enables the teacher to assume direct responsibility for influencing children's developing political attitudes through their play. The political concepts that children bring to their play—concepts of enemies and friends, good and bad, war and peace, and violence as a means of conflict resolution— come within the realm of the teacher's influence. Teachers attempt to affect these concepts at the children's level of development and interest and, by so doing, act as agents of political socialization.

For these two reasons, we feel that option 4 is the strongest one available to teachers. What is involved in implementing option 4 will vary greatly from classroom to classroom, depending on the individual children and what they bring to the classroom with respect to war play. We are not advocating that teachers develop a war play curriculum in the absence of children indicating an interest in it or that they develop this curriculum at all beyond the needs and interests of the children.

There will be some classrooms where the issue of war play will occupy a small role and the teacher will need to incorporate few of the strategies involved in implementing this option. At the same time, in such a situation the teacher will need to consider how she or he can affect what children are learning from their exposure to political issues outside the school. For those teachers who find it necessary to implement option 4 more fully, we are aware that it is a complex and difficult approach to implement and places yet another demand on teachers. It asks teachers to take on responsibility for working with children and their parents around yet another "problem" created by the society at large.

Differences Between Parents' and Teachers' Approaches to War Play

Parents' approaches to war play, we found, fell into the same four categories as those chosen by teachers, but there was one important difference between the choices of the two groups. Even though many parents also expressed discomfort and concern about the war play dilemma, more parents chose to allow the play in some form (choosing option 2 or 3) than did teachers. Even many of the parents who initially tried to ban war play said that they eventually allowed it in some form because they could see that their children wanted to and seemed to need to play this way. While we do not have a large enough sample to draw any definitive conclusions, it is interesting to speculate about what might account for this apparent difference between teachers' and parents' choices.

The different roles that parents and teachers have with respect to children and society, and the different emphases of their interactions with children, may help account for the differences we found. Parents are responsible for individual children and can base their responses on the "particular" needs of their individual child (Lightfoot, 1978). As they observe their children and identify particular interests and needs, they can modify their attitudes and responses. Teachers, on the other hand, are responsible to groups of children and to society and often base their responses on the more "universal" needs and interests of groups and society (Lightfoot, 1978). They are less likely to have the opportunity to focus on individuals' responses and needs than are parents. They generally view the needs of the individual in the context of the group and are less likely to sacrifice the potential needs of the group for the needs of individuals. Thus, parents are more able and likely to develop rules and policies with respect to war play that respond to the needs and interests their children express; that is, they are more likely to come down on the developmental side of the war play debate. Teachers, on the other hand, are more able and likely to develop rules and policies that address their responsibilities to the group and society, coming down on the sociopolitical side of the debate.

But, as with teachers, when parents choose to freely allow, place limits upon, or ban war play, without taking an active role in their children's play, they are not necessarily accomplishing what they intend to do or should do—foster children's development or political socialization as adequately as they might. At best, they are leaving development and political socialization as it relates to war play to chance; at worst, they are denying certain of their children's developmental needs and are leaving important aspects of political socialization to agents outside the home.

As with teachers, we feel that option 4, actively working with war play, is the best choice available to parents for resolving the war play dilemma. Because of the one-to-one intimate relationship parents have with their children, they are often in the best position to engage in an ongoing dialogue about war play, war toys, and violence; to share personal feelings about guns and violence; and to provide many opportunities for their children to experience cooperation and nonviolence. Therefore, we hope that, as teachers consider the difficult task of working with war play in their classrooms, they will think about how to include parents in their efforts.

Let us next look more closely at (1) what is involved in putting this option into practice, (2) the classroom context in which it might best occur, and (3) how parents and teachers might work together to solve the war play dilemma.

CHAPTER 6

Guidelines for Working with War Play

If teachers decide to choose Option 4 and work with war play in the classroom, they should be making a commitment to becoming involved in and out of the play with how children work on the developmental and political issues that arise in the play. War play cannot optimally foster development and political understanding without being considered within the whole context in which it is occurring. Young children do not separate what happens in one arena in the classroom from other arenas. And, because children learn best through concrete and direct experience, teachers will need to create a total environment that serves as a model, both in and out of the war play, for the concepts, values, and skills they hope to help children develop. Therefore, a true commitment to promoting the learnings of war play means a reexamination of the total classroom and the many other aspects that have an impact on children's emerging political understanding.

The entire classroom context in which war play occurs needs to reflect the nonauthoritarian and nonmilitaristic values and ideas that teachers hope will gradually become a part of the political attitudes and concepts children construct (Carlsson-Paige & Levin, 1985; Wolf, 1986). Children need to know that they are respected as individuals—that their thoughts, feelings, and needs will be heard and responded to. They need to experience their environment as a predictable and safe place—as a place where they can learn to understand and predict the consequences of their own and others' actions, and where they know that the teacher is ultimately in control (Isaacs, 1937; Kamii & DeVries, 1978, 1980). They need to see and learn about how positive social relationships work—how their own conflicts can be resolved peacefully, how to begin to take the point of view of another, how to begin to cooperate with others in mutually beneficial ways.

Every teacher will develop his or her own classroom curriculum and context based on personal values and educational philosophy, the needs and interests of the children in the class, and the community of which they are both a part. At the same time, while there is still much to be learned about how to work with the issues that arise in war play both within and outside of the play, some general conclusions can be reached. Drawing on our earlier discussion of child development and political socialization, we offer the following nine guidelines as a base from which teachers can begin making decisions about how to work with war play in the classroom.

Guideline 1

Develop an appreciation of the developmental and political issues individual children are working on in their war and weapons play.

The first step in working with children around their war and weapons play is to learn as much as possible about what individual children are expressing about their needs, developmental issues, political concepts, and concerns. This is important because teachers need to be able to match their efforts at affecting children's war play and political learning with the developmental concepts and issues children are working on. Thus, what teachers learn from children can serve as a guide for deciding how to facilitate play and learning (Kamii & De-Vries, 1978).

STRATEGIES

Make observations and use questions that will give information about

• The major developmental issues a child is working on in war play (e.g., control and power, separation, fantasy and reality, gender identification)
• The level of cognitive understanding revealed by a child's play (e.g., the degree of egocentrism, the ability to take the view of others, the nature of cause-and-effect connections)
• The political concepts a child is using (e.g., the nature of enemies, of conflict resolution, of death and killing)
• The nature of the images a child is using in the play (e.g., the kinds of characters portrayed, which may be taken from television or stories or be of the child's own invention; the kinds of weapons used, whether commercial, imaginary, or self-made)

- The degree to which a child is imitating and repeating a particular script over and over or creating and elaborating the play over time
- The quantity of time that a child spends engaged in war play in relation to other forms of sociodramatic play, as well as in relation to other activities and interests
- The degree to which the content of a child's war play, especially militaristic content, carries over into the child's behavior outside of play
- The areas in the play of individual children as well as the group that are likely to require teacher guidance and support to maintain emotional and physical safety of the child and group

Guideline 2

Help children develop both the quality of their war play and their political understanding within *the play.*

Although children need to be in charge of their own play in order for it to meet their needs optimally, as with other forms of dramatic play, there are many ways teachers can facilitate the play without interfering in it. The teacher's role in influencing the quality of the play is especially important with war play, because so much of the content is stereotyped, imitative, and violent; and because so much of the process is repetitive and static. At the same time, there is a fine line between facilitating and intruding; teachers have to assess continuously the impact of their interventions on children and their play.

STRATEGIES

- Base interventions on the developmental issues children are working on in their play. For instance, if a child tends to be confusing the fantasy of the play with reality, the teacher should be there to clarify the boundary. A teacher might say, "Remember, Matt, Kyle is only pretending to be the bad guy; he isn't really bad."
- Base interventions on the cognitive understanding revealed by individual children as they play. For instance, if a child does not make obvious connections between his actions and their effects as he plays, the teacher can point out to him the consequences of his behavior: "If you jump from that platform, you'll hurt yourself. Remember what happened yesterday when you tried it."
- Foster political knowledge in ways that build on the political

concepts revealed in the play. For example, if a group of children always only portray the "bad guy" as attacking them, the teacher might try to expand their concept of the enemy: "Where does that bad guy go when he's not fighting with you?"

• Bring in new content for the play, such as new props, roles, and physical settings, which grow out of the current content and will help children vary and elaborate the play. This is especially important for those children who seem to be following a television script or acting out the same theme over and over in the same way. For example, if children are using a particular setting in the same way day after day to repeat one play scenario, the teacher might try to change a feature of the setting by saying, "Today, the platform [which has been a space ship] is a ship in the Atlantic Ocean." The teacher also could take the children to a new setting, such as a park, to encourage them to adapt their play to the new environment.

• Help those children who seem to be inventing a lot of their own play content to maintain their originality in the midst of the more stereotypical play other children may be engaging in. Try to help incorporate the invented material of these children into the war play of the group. For instance, if a group of children is pretending that Cobra (G.I. Joe's enemy) is chasing them, the teacher can ask the one child with a personally invented monster who has magical powers, "Does your monster have a special power that can help protect the 'good guys' from Cobra?"

• Make comments to accompany the play that relate to what the children are doing (e.g., "I see you are after the bad guys again" or, "You found a new way to travel through space today"). Such comments do not necessarily intrude if the child does not want to be interrupted or channeled in a new direction. At the same time, they often elicit a commentary from the child about what she is doing. As a result the teacher may gain further insight into the child's play and get ideas about possible ways to help her elaborate it, and the child may even develop a plan for elaborating the play on her own, just by talking about what she is doing.

• Avoid placing adult value judgments on the themes that arise in the play; rather, try to talk about the themes in a way that has meaning for the child. If a child is making a magic potion to "kill the bad guy," do not say, "You shouldn't kill" or, "I do not like killing." Say something like, "Wow, that stuff looks really powerful! What's going into the potion? What else do you need to do to make it?"

• Utilize open-ended questions as an ongoing vehicle for creating the kinds of disequilibrium that can help children find new problems to solve and make new connections (Hohmann, Banet, & Weikart,

1979; Kamii & DeVries, 1978; Paley, 1984). Examples of open-ended questions are, "What can the bad guy do now that he's trapped?" "Tell me about how you made that weapon?" "How can you get Cobra to listen to you?" These can grow out of what is happening in any given moment and allow for many different responses, depending on the individual meaning the child makes of the question.

  • Whenever possible, choose interventions that have the potential to break down the stereotyped and violent political concepts children are receiving from society. Encourage a wider range of roles for males and females (e.g., "It's pretty boring to be Princess Leah all the time. What else can girls be here?"). Foster a more differentiated and human understanding of the enemy (e.g., "Oh, Cobra's hurt. Can we find him a doctor?"). Facilitate an understanding of the actual effects of aggression and violence (e.g., "I'm glad to see you and Miguel are just pretending to hit, because if you really hit each other you'll both get hurt"). Such comments illustrate how adults can convey potentially political content to young children as they play, at the concrete and immediate level that they can understand.

Guideline 3

Work with war play, and the issues and themes it raises, outside *of the play.*

  While children are actually involved in war play, they often do not want to be interrupted and either resist adults' efforts to intervene or deal only superficially with the input provided. In addition, if teachers attempt to intervene too actively or extensively, the play can become more the teachers' creation than the children's. Sometimes, stepping back and establishing a dialogue with children, *outside* of their war play, on the content used or issues raised in their play can result in a less intrusive and more meaningful discussion. Such a dialogue can help children expand their political concepts and provide them with input that will later help them develop the quality of their play. This is often a more appropriate and effective way to work with the political and social issues that are part of children's war play.

STRATEGIES

  • Use the content of children's war play to foster an understanding of conflict resolution. The issues and disagreements that arise in children's play, because they come from firsthand experiences that the children care a lot about, provide ideal material for reflection and learning. Experiences that help children predict and understand the consequences of their actions, take points of view other than their own, and consider more than one solution to a problem all contribute to the development of the skills required for successful conflict resolution (Carlsson-Paige & Levin, 1986; Kriedler, 1984; Wolf, 1986).

The teacher might take an actual conflict that arose between children in their play and raise it for discussion at a group meeting: "The 'bad guys' got very angry today when the 'good guys' tried to capture their space ship. How did the 'bad guys' ['good guys'] feel about it? What could the 'bad guys' have done besides pushing? What are some ways the 'good guys' could make a space ship of their own?" After a play scenario is over, the teacher can initiate a discussion between two children who were involved in a conflict by saying, "The two of you had a hard time deciding who would be Princess Leah. Let's think of what we can do so you'll have an easier time tomorrow." Or, the teacher might raise for discussion some of the broader social issues raised by various war play characters by saying such things as, "Rambo always seems to get what he wants by fighting. What are other ways he could get what he wants?"

• Use the content of children's war play to help them develop those political concepts that are used in their war play. Teachers can help children expand the static and dichotomous categories that often characterize the political content in their play by providing experiences that slightly contradict or extend children's current thinking.

Teachers can help children humanize the anonymous and unidimensional concept of the "enemy" that they often use in their play, by asking such questions as, "Does Cobra have a family?" "What does his family do when he's fighting?" This also can be done by suggesting activities such as, "Let's draw pictures of Cobra's family" or, "Let's build a home for Cobra's family in the block area." As children discuss such things as what Cobra likes to eat, who his friends are, and what he likes to do, they develop an increasing understanding and appreciation of the similarities and differences among people, as they are helped to break down the "we-they" dichotomy they are given by the media.

• Help children bring the content of their war play into other areas of the curriculum (Kohl, 1976). This can help children to experience new competencies and develop new interests; it can also help them deepen and extend the repertoire of symbols they are using in their war play. Symbolic representation, in its various forms, helps children construct meaning and come to a greater understanding of concepts (Elkind, Hetzel, & Coe, 1974; Hohmann et al., 1979). It also helps children progress beyond stereotyped concepts as the new representations deepen and extend meaning. We can help children find and develop new interests and new ways of representing the play content that excites them at the moment by bringing the play into the block area, the sand and water tables, and the writing and art areas.

For example, if children are using sticks as pretend walkie-talkies, the teacher could set up materials at the workbench and help the children build their own walkie-talkies. As the children work, the teacher could help them think about what functions the walkie-talkie needs to have, what materials are needed and how they can be used, and how this new instrument can be taken back into the play. In addition to helping expand the children's concept of walkie-talkie and its use in the play, this intervention could also lead to a new interest in woodworking, a growing sense of mastery with materials, and a curriculum unit around the theme of walkie-talkies.

• Develop other curriculum activities and themes that satisfy the same developmental needs met by war play. Some teachers have found that, when offered a range of images to use in meeting developmental needs through play, children may not always choose the most contemporary media images. Teachers need to provide alternative images to those offered by television and toys, but that still address such issues as mastery, power, and control and fit with the way young children view the world. There is a rich tradition of folklore and literature for young children and many possibilities for incorporating these into the curriculum. Teachers may find that children need help in pulling away from the attraction of powerful, ready-made media images. Children also may need help elaborating the less concrete images that come from other sources (e.g., a book), in order to use them meaningfully in their play.

Teachers can develop curriculum based on books such as *Where the Wild Things Are* (Sendak, 1963) and stories such as *The Wizard of Oz* (Baum, 1979), to provide powerful alternative models for working out developmental concerns. One kindergarten teacher told us that her classroom was dominated by repetitive and aggressive "Star Wars" play, so she began reading the story of *The Wizard of Oz* at group time. She filled the dramatic play area of the classroom with props relating to the story. In class discussions of the story, she placed special emphasis on the issues that related to the concerns she felt children were expressing in their "Star Wars" play (e.g., power, control, and autonomy). She told us how the children gradually became immersed in playing out, drawing, and making props for the story of *The Wizard of*

Oz, while at the same time the "Star Wars" play gradually diminished. (See Appendix II, "Two Sample Curriculum Webs.")

In addition to using books and stories, teachers can develop curriculum units on such themes as scary things, monsters, dinosaurs, and creatures from outer space. (See Appendix II, Web 2.) Such topics also appeal to many of the same developmental needs and interests children express in their war play (Kohl, 1976; Seefeldt & Tinney, 1985).

Guideline 4

Develop strategies for keeping the play safe and manageable in the classroom.

Children learn best in environments where they feel safe and in control (Isaacs, 1937). Teachers have to provide environments in which children can trust that they are safe, or too much of their energy will go into protecting themselves, inhibiting their becoming involved in productive activities (Kostelnik et al., 1986).

Because children's war and weapons play involves working out issues of power and control, it can often become scary and unpredictable for some children. For the children who are working on impulse control through their war play, there is the constant risk of losing control. For those children who are less involved in the war play or are more in control, there can be the threat of being "shot at" or actually hit by other children. Both groups of children need to trust that the teacher can protect them and keep them safe from the loss of their own or others' control. Therefore, teachers need to think through how they will work with children in an ongoing way to create a safe context in which war play can occur.

STRATEGIES

• Before war play becomes a part of the classroom, decide on the few basic limits that will help keep the play safe. As children gain experience with these limits and the need for new limits arises, they will be able to discuss and modify them with more concrete understanding of the possible implications of each (see Paley, 1984).

• Use the same norms that guide general classroom behavior for guiding behavior during war play. Although war play can give rise to aggressive and violent behaviors, children are most likely to learn how to control their behavior when they draw on the rules that they have learned in situations where it is easier to maintain self-control. For instance, if there is a rule that children respect one another's work, and a child pretending he is He-Man destroys the "enemy's" cave built in sand, the teacher should rely on the shared norm in explaining why the behavior is unacceptable.

• When limits need to be set or conflicts arise, and there is no danger of anyone getting hurt, help children become actively involved in working out their own problems. As children gain experience in working out the acceptable standards for their play and behavior with other children and adults, they become better able to take responsibility for their own behavior and regulate their play. Rather than jumping in and providing a necessary limit, teachers should help children step back and evaluate the effectiveness of existing rules as well as consider possibilities for new rules. For example, a teacher may say to children, "We had all agreed that you could use the large Tinkertoys as a pretend sword, but Eli got hit. What are we going to do about it?" This teacher would need to work with the children until they found an appropriate solution. At the same time, it may be useful for children to be able to try some of their own "imperfect" solutions (those that may not seem sensible by adult logic), so they can see how their own ideas work out in practice and learn to improve upon them (Paley, 1984).

• When intervention is needed, try to enter into the war play in ways that do not stop it; help children work out solutions that give them a safe alternative for continuing their play. For instance, when play is deteriorating because two children both want the "fantasy cape," rather than saying, "You need to share or stop playing," the teacher can say, "I know how you can share it! I have an hour glass, and I'll show you how to use it to take turns."

• When limits are needed, try not to place adult value judgments on the children's war play. For example, when a child hits another child, rather than saying, "It's bad to hit; stop it right now," a teacher might say, "Even if Howie is pretending to be the 'bad guy,' when you hit him he gets hurt, and I can't let you do that." Such an adult response helps children decenter and learn about the effects of their actions, rather than feel guilty or bad about themselves.

• If the only way to insure children's sense of safety is to stop the play, then the teacher must do so.

Guideline 5

Decide what role war toys and weapons will have in the classroom.

When teachers decide to include war play in their curriculum, they will have to confront many issues related to war toys. We feel it is crucial for teachers to develop policies for the classroom that both take into account their own goals to foster development and nonviolent attitudes and also respond to the needs and interests that children have.

Teachers have to juggle many conflicting factors as they begin to figure out an approach to war toys in the classroom. It can be a very difficult task, at best, and one that few teachers tell us they feel they have totally resolved. At the same time, several basic underlying factors have proven helpful for guiding teachers as they attempt to evolve an approach to weapons and war toys that feels comfortable to them and responds to the needs and interests of the particular individuals in their class.

STRATEGIES

• Permit war toys of any kind only if children's sense of safety in the classroom can be maintained. Young children have an easier time making pretend weapons than playing with them. A child can make a pretend gun with Bristle Blocks, but, when he starts using it as a weapon in play, a whole new set of difficulties arises. The play is often more intense and emotional when weapons are involved, and children lose control more easily. Because of the way that young children think, a gun can suddenly take on the power and destructive capacity that it symbolizes. It is possible to allow weapons in the classroom with different kinds of restrictions. Some children may be able to make weapons in small-worlds play, for example, but not use them in fantasy play. Other children may be able to use them in fantasy play with a "no shooting each other" rule. Still others may be able to pretend to shoot at each other if it's agreed to by both parties in advance. If a classroom succeeds in using pretend weapons for play while maintaining a sense of safety for every child, it usually is only after a long process of working together and working out play situations with weapons in which every child feels secure.

• Work toward a policy of banning commercial weapons from the play. It is important to differentiate between single-purpose, commercially made war toys and war toys that children make out of open-ended materials. Because single-purpose toys are so specific in what they do (e.g., shoot bullets), they define for children how they should be used (i.e., to kill) and determine how a child plays with them. To the extent that these toys are tied to television programs, they tend to define and limit play even further. War toys made from open-ended materials such as clay, blocks, or Legos are better because they allow children to use them in a whole variety of ways based on their developmental level and interests. When children make their own weapons from such materials, they tend to define the attributes of the weapons and how they are to be used. Ten children making guns with Legos can make ten different creations to be used in ten different ways; ten children playing with Rambo dolls and the accompanying weapons are likely to play in very similar ways. It is probably for this reason that most teachers prefer to fill their classrooms with open-ended materials, rather than commercial, single-purpose toys of any kind; however, this is especially true of war toys because of the many other negative values adults associate with them.

On the other hand, children love these single-purpose combat toys; they are very seductive and many children have them. Teachers need to stay in touch with children's pressing interests and with their lives outside of school. Because these toys are affecting children's development and their early political ideas, teachers need to play a role in influencing the effects of these toys on children. Also, teachers need to work together with parents, many of whom are experiencing tremendous pressure and guilt about buying these toys for their children; teachers have to figure out ways of building onto what parents are doing in positive ways.

Teachers can convey an attitude of acceptance toward children's favorite toys while minimizing the role these toys have in school. For example, there can be a particular time of day when children can use commercial toys (such as the first hour of school), or there can be a particular place in the room where they can be used (such as the dramatic play area), or a particular activity during which they may be introduced (such as group sharing). At the same time, teachers can encourage children to create the props they need for their play. If a child says that he needs his G.I. Joe during play time, the teacher can say, "What else could we use to make people—clay, or the small colored cubes?" Or, "Luis made a wonderful warship with Legos yesterday. Maybe he'll have some ideas about how to make what you want." It may take some children a long time to learn to use open-ended materials to create props for their war play because they are so accustomed to the prescribed features of ready-made toys.

• Help children move beyond the single-purpose violence associated with war toys. When a child uses an object such as a finger or Legos to make a weapon during war play, the initial focus for using the weapon is usually on violence and killing. For many children, this is often where the play with weapons gets stuck, and it can cause many problems with other children who get hurt or upset. It is also often the aspect of weapons play that is most disturbing to the teacher. By helping children get beyond this focus, the teacher can help them expand their play and learning and avoid conflicts with other children.

For example, a child may make a Lego gun and begin shooting it at another child. The teacher can say, "Tell me how your gun works?" thereby finding out the meaning the gun has for the child. If the child were to describe the gun as one that has bullets and kills people, the teacher could say something like, "What would happen to the bad guy if your gun shot glue instead of bullets?" Or the teacher might ask, "Could this gun catch people in a different way so they would be captured, not killed?" If such questions aroused the child's interest, they could lead the child to begin to focus on ways of redesigning and/or redefining the weapon, or they might lead the child to focus more on what will happen to the captured people (e.g., build a "prison" with blocks).

Such an intervention, when it works, achieves several things. It helps the child move beyond the notion of the single-purpose violent weapon and to expand her involvement in working with materials. It gets her thinking about how to become involved in the issues associated with good-guy/bad-guy play in ways that go beyond a single focus on violence and killing.

An alternative, when this approach does not work, is to state clearly what is allowed, while giving the child an alternative way of using the toy. For instance, in the preceding situation, if the child continued to shoot bullets to kill, the teacher might say, "It is not all right to shoot at Maria when she doesn't want you to. You can shoot at the monster by the tree or you can find someone who is willing to play with you this way."

• Outside of the play, find ways of creating a political context for the weapons and of developing in the children concepts of weapons that go beyond killing. Have discussions about the weapons that came up in the play. For instance, if a child makes a Lego gun that shoots glue, bring it to a meeting and talk about its special quality and the interesting effects it can have. Do a movement activity where children get stuck in the glue, which gradually hardens. A teacher may mention how it's nice to find weapons that can do interesting things, not just kill. This exposes the children to the teacher's values about killing with weapons, but does so in the context of the children's interests.

When commercial combat toys come into the classroom for

"show and tell" (which can be one good way of curtailing their use in school without banning them totally), use them as an opportunity to help children expand their use of them as well as learn about their negative qualities. For instance, you could say, "Poor Rambo. He only has one way of solving all of his problems. Let's help him. What else could he do?" This can also be a time for discussing your own feelings about the toys and for reinforcing the different policies the children's parents have adopted with respect to these toys.

Guideline 6

Work toward helping children expand beyond the stereotyped sex-role behavior that arises in war play.

More and more, war play is an issue that tends to divide girls from boys. Boys have always been more interested in this play than girls, but the current societal context tends to solidify this difference in interest and to do so at an earlier age. Vivian Paley, an author and kindergarten teacher for many years, states, "I am certain that superhero play begins at an earlier age than it did thirty years ago and that the boys leave the doll corner at least a year ahead of schedule" (1984, p. 108). As boys become more involved in aggressive warlike play at an earlier age, they are less likely to interact with girls. This early segregation, as well as the deep involvement of many boys in war play, can cause alienation and fear between the sexes and a narrowing of the range of behaviors and interests that children of both sexes develop. This can have potentially important effects on children's overall development as well as on their developing political attitudes.

It is important for teachers to consider how to break down the divisions that war play can create between boys and girls, to help boys to expand their stereotyped behavior, and to find ways of making the play more accessible to girls. At the same time, we want to assist both groups in learning to expand the range of behaviors and attitudes involved in their play.

STRATEGIES

• Engage in dialogues with boys and girls about the sex-role stereotypes present in their play and the sex-role models they are given. Teachers can utilize the direct experiences of children to foster reflection, evaluation, and problem solving about sex roles. For example, a teacher might begin a group discussion by asking such questions as, "Let's look at all the things that Rambo can do. Is he like the men that you know? What other things do the men you know do?" Questions like these can encourage children to relate their own experiences with fathers and other men to media and toy images of "maleness." Such a discussion can also help children who engage in Rambo play to bring new ideas of "maleness" to their play. Asking children what they think would happen if for a week only girls could go in the block area and only boys could go in the house corner, or if for a week the house and block areas were combined, could lead to an interesting discussion about why there is often segregation between the sexes in play or why boys and girls often choose to play in different areas of the room.

• Try to find ways of helping girls become involved in the play that go beyond the roles that are generally assumed by boys. In general, girls are allowed a wider range of behaviors than boys (e.g., it is easier for a girl to be a "tomboy" than for a boy to be a "sissy"), and therefore it may be easier for girls to be incorporated into war play than for boys to become part of house play. We know of several cases where boys who attempted to become involved in the doll corner were "shamed" out by other boys (e.g., "Boys don't give babies baths!"). At the same time, boys often attempt to exclude from their war play girls who try to join in. Teachers can find nondictatorial ways of helping girls become a part of the play. For instance, we saw a situation where a group of boys were building a village in outer space for the space invaders who were going around attacking earth people. The boys told a girl who asked to join in that she was not strong enough to build the village. The teacher came up and asked the boys about their village. She saw that they were using rocks. She suggested that the girl could be the rock collector. Everyone quickly agreed, and soon several girls and then also boys were going around the playground putting rocks into a wheelbarrow. Such an approach avoided directly confronting the boys' stereotype that "girls are weaker" but at the same time gave the girls a job that was seen as using "strength." It also helped involve the girls in ways that emphasized the building of a city rather than the violence of the space invaders and helped the girls and boys interact.

• Work to find appropriate ways of helping girls meet some of the same needs boys are meeting as they engage in war play and to help boys meet some of the same needs girls meet in their nonwar dramatic play. Boys often use their war play to feel powerful and strong. Girls also need an opportunity to experience such feelings. Teachers can use a variety of classroom situations to encourage these feelings in girls. When a girl lifts up a heavy piece of equipment in the classroom, the teacher can point out her strength. When a girl is playing mother and rescues the children from a danger, the teacher can point out that child's power and bravery.

Boys also need help getting beyond the strong, powerful figures they imitate. Such behaviors can often be used to mask boys' feelings of helplessness and insecurity (Paley, 1984). The boys who are most passionately involved in war play are often the boys who are most insecure and in need of the most support in learning to express and act out a range of feelings. As more and more of boys' play focuses on acting out these aggressive roles to the exclusion of the more nurturing and feeling roles experienced in other forms of dramatic play (e.g., the doll corner), boys may have less and less opportunity to express and work out feelings of vulnerability and uncertainty. Teachers can help boys learn to express a wider range of feelings, in and out of their play. For instance, when a child involved in play is actually hurt, angry, or afraid, the teacher can matter-of-factly point out that child's feelings to the other children involved and help the children learn to respond to these feelings in nonaggressive ways. For example, when Seymour is about to attack Marcus, who has broken his Lego gun, the teacher can say, "Seymour is angry and upset because Marcus broke the gun he worked hard to build. What can we do to help Seymour feel better so he doesn't feel like hitting?" This brings feelings other than power and strength into the play, gives legitimacy to them, and helps children focus on their ability to help others in nurturing ways. Similar results are accomplished by saying, "Henry is crying because you scared him when you all started running toward him growling. You were very scary monsters. Henry was trying to be a baby monster, and all kinds of babies get scared by big noises. Who can think of a big noise that scared you when you were a baby?"

• Encourage interaction and friendship between girls and boys, in and out of the play. As segregation between boys and girls does occur as a result of war play, and as girls and boys interact less with each other in their dramatic play in general, friendships and interactions in other areas of the classroom and out of school are also likely to become more segregated at an earlier age. Forcing children to interact with each other when they do not choose to is not likely to result in meaningful, sustained interactions, but ways can be found to help them interact around mutual self-interest, or shared interests or concerns. If the boys have set up a hospital for their injured superheroes and a baby (i.e., a girl) in the house corner is sick, the teacher can suggest that "the baby be taken to the hospital." If a boy wants to make a sign about saving the block building he has made for He-Man and a girl is good at writing, the teacher can direct the boy to her to help make his sign. If a boy and girl share similar family experiences (e.g., a new baby) or similar cultural backgrounds (e.g., both speak Spanish at home), the teacher can have them share their experiences with the new babies with the class or work with them to prepare Spanish "lessons" for the class. By so doing, the teacher can help boys and girls find concrete and meaningful ways of interacting that occur for reasons that grow out of the children's interests and experiences, rather than the teacher's decrees.

• Those boys who do not demonstrate a deep interest in war play should be supported against the pressures of the peer group and their ideas and interests be utilized. There will be boys who, for a variety of reasons (e.g., lack of need, exposure, or interest), will not be as caught up in war play as many of the other boys in the class. The boys who are more involved in war play can exert a great deal of both direct and indirect pressure to get these boys to join in the more aggressive war play of the group (Paley, 1984). The teacher can help the range of interests represented by the boys in the class become a part of the curriculum. If Mario is interested in doctor play because one of his parents is a doctor, setting up a hospital where the "injured" superheroes can go to be treated by Dr. Mario can help Mario become a part of the play of the boys while both maintaining his own nonwar play interest and helping the war play–focused boys to expand their play into more nurturing and diverse roles.

• Find ways to facilitate and convey a sense of interest in the girls' nonwar dramatic play as the war play curriculum is developed in the classroom. The dramatic play engaged in by girls often does not place the kinds of demands on the teacher's time and energy that boys' war play or other dramatic play can. Teachers tend to spend more time interacting with boys than girls in general (Sadker & Sadker, 1985). As teachers begin to take an active role in facilitating war play rather than just allowing and managing it or enforcing a ban, it can become very easy for the teacher to lose sight of the house corner altogether. It is important that teachers continue to value and facilitate the girls' dramatic play and to help girls expand beyond the stereotyped female behavior that can often occur in it.

• Present a variety of attractive, powerful, and humanistic role models to boys and girls, to provide alternatives to those that typify war play. The issue of providing children with models that go beyond the aggressive and militaristic models often presented in the media and by toys has already been discussed. Providing alternative models of both males and females whom children can use in their play and discussions, such as Peter Pan and Wendy, Dorothy in *The Wizard of Oz*, Cinderella, and Desmond in *Desmond and the Monsters* (Althea, 1975), can help both boys and girls find ways of acting powerful and strong in nonmilitaristic ways.

Guideline 7

Assume the role of researcher in the ongoing process of working with war play.

The curriculum of a center or school where teachers have decided to work actively with children's war play can be greatly enhanced when teachers become "action" researchers (Elliott, 1976; Heck & Williams, 1984; Philadelphia Teachers' Learning Cooperative, 1984). Collecting data from the parents and teachers regarding their ideas and feelings about war play can provide a useful basis from which to begin. Once the curriculum is in progress, collecting data on an ongoing basis can serve as a guide for deciding how various approaches are working and for continuing to develop new strategies for how best to proceed.

STRATEGIES

• Develop questionnaires to be completed by staff members and parents. The data collected can help teachers identify the range of views represented among the adults involved and pinpont areas of potential agreement and disagreement among staff members and between the staff and parents. The questionnaires in Appendix I provide suggestions for possible questions to include.

• Keep ongoing records about what actually happens once the play begins to occur in the classroom. Such records can serve many purposes. They can help teachers identify recurrent themes and see how the play progresses over time. They can assist teachers in reflecting on the effectiveness of their own roles in working with the play and in formulating new strategies for increasing their effectiveness. Information collected on individual children can serve as a basis for working to meet individual needs more appropriately or for working with the children's parents. Specific issues that emerge from the records can be shared at staff meetings as a way for individual teachers to get peer feedback and assess the overall impact and effectiveness of the school's efforts. There are many forms the records can take. Curriculum webs offer one format for recording themes that interest the children (see Appendix II). Anecdotal records, brief recording sheets, or an ongoing diary are formats teachers may find it helpful to use in keeping running records on individual children (see Appendix III, "Two Record-Keeping Formats").

• Have staff members observe each other as they begin to work with children's war play. The information that a colleague records while observing another teacher can help teachers to step back and look at what is occurring with the play and with their role in relation to it, and to open up possibilities for change. This approach can also help create an ongoing support system for teachers as they discuss the observations with each other.

Guideline 8

Create an ongoing dialogue with parents about their children's war and weapons play.

In any classroom, teachers will find a whole range of sentiments among parents about the issue of war play. Many parents have concerns and questions and experience confusion about their children's involvement in war play. They also often have strong opinions about how they would like war play to be approached with their children, both at school and at home. In addition, as teachers attempt to facilitate war play actively in their classrooms, parents are likely to have many questions as well as potential disagreements about the teacher's approach.

Therefore teachers have a responsibility to engage in an ongoing dialogue with parents about war play. They need to familiarize themselves with the approach to war play parents take with their children and to explain what is being done in school and why. Through a dialogue that helps parents better understand the issues underlying the war play dilemma and the rationale for the teacher's approach, parents will often be better prepared to support what is happening at school and to make informed decisions about how they will respond to war play at home. At the same time, teachers will have a clearer idea about how the school program can connect with what happens at home and how the classroom approach should be modified or changed, based on the input provided by parents. In addition, when disagreements do arise between parents and the teacher, the climate of give and take established by the dialogue will make it more possible to come up with an approach that everyone feels they have had a part in creating (Fisher, 1981).

STRATEGIES

• Create formal and informal opportunities for engaging in dialogues with parents about attitudes and approaches to war play. Plan parents' nights where teachers and parents can discuss their approaches to war play and the reasons for it. Arrange for parent observations in the classroom, where parents have an opportunity to see their children's war play and the teacher's role in it. Give appropriate articles to read to parents who request additional information about war play. Share the particular nature of individual children's involvement in war play at parent conferences, through classroom displays about the war play curriculum (e.g., photographs of structures made for superhero figures in the block corner), and when parents come to the class to drop off or pick up their children. Because educational settings vary a great deal as to the amount of regular contact parents and teachers are able to have, teachers will need to develop channels of communication that are most responsive to the parents at their site.

• Adapt what happens in the classroom, based on the information obtained from discussions with parents. The classroom approach chosen by the teacher will be affected by the experiences of the children in the classroom. For example, the degree to which children watch television, the degree to which commercial war toys are a part of their play at home, and the range of parent attitudes about the play will all affect the way a teacher works with individual children and the group.

• Help parents feel supported and empowered with respect to their own roles and responsibilities in their children's war play. Teachers can help parents feel that they have a place to come where they can discuss their feelings and concerns about war play and talk through solutions. And, as appropriate, teachers can help parents learn to facilitate their own children's war play actively. Most of the guidelines for teachers can be easily adapted for parent use. As parents begin to discuss and become involved actively in their children's war play, they are likely to begin to feel more in control of their own feelings about this play and the influences that affect their children's lives.

Guideline 9

Develop an understanding of your own feelings about war and violence, as separate from the views and needs of children.

Before teachers can fully respond to children, it is important for them to be able to look at children in as unbiased a way as possible.

Teachers continually have to insure that they are not confusing their own feelings with the child's perspective and imposing their own adult views on children. With an emotional topic like war play in a war-permeated world, this is a difficult and ongoing process. If teachers are concerned about the influences of society on children's war play and the militaristic concepts that might result, then they need to find ways outside of the classroom to express and work out these feelings and to become involved in attempting to affect the societal context that is causing the changes in the play.

STRATEGIES

• Establish channels for dialogue with colleagues who share the same concerns. For instance, we know of one small elementary school where the entire faculty meets on a regular basis to discuss how well school policies and classroom practices around permitting war play are meeting children's and adults' needs, as well as to modify existing policy based on the discussion.
• Engage in political activity outside of the classroom on behalf of children, such as working to influence the societal circumstances that are directly affecting children's war play. There are many social and political action groups that are working to affect society on behalf of children; they can provide clearly defined starting points for teachers who desire to take this route (see Appendix IV, "Annotated List of Organizations").

CHAPTER 7

Can We Solve the War Play Dilemma?

Children have engaged in war and weapons play for generations. This form of play helps children work on issues that are basic to their development; it also helps them construct early concepts about their world, some of which are of a political nature. Society, by the images and models it provides, helps children define the content they will use in their war play; what changes over time is the content that society offers. As this content changes, the concepts children construct can change. Today, the images and models children are using in their play are greatly influenced by television and toys, and are becoming increasingly violent and militaristic.

These violent images penetrate classrooms and homes often against the wishes of adults. In many of the interviews we conducted, teachers and parents described their attempts to limit war play. Teachers who banned the play talked about the underworld that developed as children tried to continue their war play outside of the teacher's view—the G.I. Joe game carried on in whispers in the reading loft, the action figures pulled out of pockets under the platform on the playground. Parents who tried to curb their children's war play talked about the difficulty of maintaining this position as their children became exposed to violent television programs and war toys from many different directions. They said it was impossible to avoid the inundation of violent images—on pajamas, on lunch boxes, in toy advertisements enclosed in the Sunday paper.

Along with expressing their own lack of control, both teachers and parents often looked to one another to do something to improve the situation. In many interviews, teachers and other professionals criticized parents for allowing their children to watch violent programs on television and for buying them the accompanying toys. They called upon parents to "just turn the television off" and "draw the line" with their children. And often parents pointed the finger at schools as the source of their child's first interest in violent play, with such comments as, "My son never heard of G.I. Joe until he went to school." In addition, both teachers and parents often charged that toy manufacturers and television programmers were responsible for children's current preoccupation with war play.

In responding to such charges, representatives of the toy industry frequently assert that the marketplace governs toy manufacturing patterns. They argue that the public buys what it likes; the industry only responds to those preferences. Television producers voice a similar perspective: that the producers' incentive is to create shows that will be watched. In both cases, the criterion is whether or not the product is "in demand" and will sell. But from society's perspective, the situation is more complicated than toy and television industry representatives suggest.

We have tried to construct a picture of how war play and war toys as they currently exist may be having negative effects on children's development and political thinking. Any such negative effects represent costs to society that are not reflected in the industries' profit-and-loss calculations and thus do not guide their decisions. When the true costs to society are not fully reflected in costs to producers, there are compelling grounds for public sector intervention into the marketplace. Thus we are faced with serious questions for public policy regarding children's television programming and advertising and the role of the Federal Communications Commission and the Federal Trade Commission.

Other countries, because of concerns about the detrimental effects of war toys on children's development and attitudes, have taken steps to limit or eliminate these toys. In Sweden, for example, the sale of war toys is prohibited. A voluntary agreement among the National Board for Consumer Policies, the Swedish Council for Children's Play, and the toy trade organizations was reached in 1979. The agreement stated that sale of all toys, games, and model kits depicting modern warfare from 1914 onward, including mail-order products, would be discontinued. Finland provides a second example: On October 2, 1986, an agreement was signed in Helsinki by the National Board for Commerce and Industry, the National Board for Social Welfare, and the Entrepreneurs for Toy and Hobby Equipment Manufacturing; its terms stipulate that, effective January 1, 1987, all parties will refrain from manufacturing, importing, and selling war toys.

Both of these policy steps were taken within the context of a much larger analysis of what constitutes a healthy toy and play environment for children. The Swedish Council for Children's Play, founded by the Swedish government in 1971, is responsible for making Swedes aware of the importance of play in children's development and for promoting materials, toys, and facilities that provide positive play opportunities. Likewise, the agreement signed in Helsinki was part of a larger agreement to promote research and information that would serve to enhance the development of toy and play culture in Finland. Perhaps we in the United States need to ask ourselves what kind of a society we want to offer our children and how we can best convey that to them.

Where does all of this leave teachers who are facing the war play dilemma? Despite their frequent feelings of powerlessness about war play and war toys, there are things that teachers can do. They can allow children to bring their war play into the classroom, and actively work with the play and the issues that arise out of it. By so doing, teachers can facilitate children's optimal development through play and foster nonmilitaristic political values and concepts. Teachers can also open up discussions with parents about their children's war play and work toward trying out a similar approach at home. But both teachers and parents can also exert a parallel effort in the area of public policy. Both groups are needed to take the many steps that will be required in order to draw attention to the need for dialogue and change regarding social policies that affect the quality of children's lives and perhaps the future of society.

Appendixes

References

Index

Sample Questionnaires and Summary of Responses

Summary of Parent, Teacher, and Child Data

The data we obtained from questionnaires and interviews helped us begin to construct a picture of the nature and range of teachers' and parents' current attitudes, concerns, and approaches with respect to war play. Our sample was neither of sufficient size nor of a systematic enough nature to provide quantitative information about the current attitudes about war play that can be generalized to the population at large. Much more systematic and extensive research is needed than is reported here, to be able to do this, as well as to document the possible effects current war play practices are having on children's development and political understanding. We will discuss the results in each category first, and print sample questionnaires afterward.

DATA FROM PARENTS

Parent Questionnaire Data. Data from parents were collected using questionnaires and interviews. Questionnaires were distributed to the parents of three- to five-year-old children attending four daycare centers. The centers, all in Massachusetts, were chosen so as to represent as much diversity as possible. Two were urban centers, one of which had children from primarily middle- and upper-income families and the other of which had children from primarily low-income families who represented a great deal of ethnic and cultural diversity. The third center was suburban, with children primarily from blue-collar families. The fourth center was rural and had children from a wide range of economic backgrounds.

Of a total of 120 questionnaires distributed, 59 (49%) were completed. The response rate was much higher for parents of boys (N = 42) than for girls (N = 17), even though girls and boys were represented about equally in the population. In general, the boys' questionnaires were completed in greater detail and depth than girls' questionnaires. Only five parents of girls indicated their daughters attempted to engage in war play and then usually when they wanted to play with boys; and no parents of girls expressed any concern about their child's involvement in the play.

On the other hand, all but three parents of boys reported their sons did engage in war play, and these three parents banned the play. Of those parents with sons who engaged in war play, more than two-thirds expressed some degree of discomfort. Two-thirds of the parents indicated they either saw the play as a necessary part of children's development in general or as meeting the specific needs of their particular children. With respect to parents' approaches to dealing with their sons' war play (in overlapping categories), one-half had established specific limits, which they seemed to enforce regularly, and another one-half attempted to express their own feelings about the play to their children or find ways to infuse their own values into and around the play. Other approaches reflected in parents' responses included redirecting the play when possible to some other activity; trying to serve as less violent role models within the play; ignoring the play; and getting angry. Three-quarters of the parents allowed toy guns and weapons and/or action figures in the home; those who did not often mentioned "child-made" weapons as acceptable. With respect to the sources and content of the play, two-thirds of the parents described television and/or commercial war toy themes as present in their sons' war play and all but three parents felt the play was influenced by television. Almost two-thirds of the parents described at least some of their sons' war play in ways that made it sound imitative of current television images. From most to least, television, school, older male siblings, and neighbors were listed by parents as the sources of their sons' first interest in war play. Parents who could remember when the play first began indicated its onset from as early as eighteen months to as late as three years of age.

Parent Interview Data. Thirty interviews were conducted with parents. The questions were of an open-ended nature, and no consistent format was followed. The goal of these interviews was to explore the range of parents' attitudes, feelings, and approaches to war play and to gain perspective on recent changes in the play. While the same general questions were asked of all parents in interviews as in the questionnaires, in the interviews there was more room to explore the issues that were of individual concern. Among those parents interviewed (in overlapping categories) were (1) grandparents who described their own approaches to war play with their children as well as their children's current approaches with their grandchildren; (2) parents of children who were both over ten and younger than six years old (to obtain comparisons between their older and younger children's war play); and (3) parents from a variety of geographical locations including Iowa, Colorado, Canada, and Sweden, and backgrounds including conscientious objectors and Vietnam War veterans. The sample was weighted toward parents of boys rather than girls, and toward parents from middle-income groups and higher educational levels than the general population, but a wide range of economic and educational levels was represented.

While it is more difficult to quantify the interview data than the questionnaire data because of its more open-ended nature, parents' responses from the interviews reflected patterns similar to those obtained from the questionnaires. One difference that stood out in the interviews was how much most parents wanted to talk about their thoughts and feelings about their children's war play, their desire for guidance, and the degree to which they seemed to be upset about but finding their own ways to adapt to the current situation. The interviews also captured in greater detail than the questionnaires how often parents' ideas about war play changed as they struggled to work out war play policies with their children and how often war play had crept into their homes in ways over which they felt they had little control. Finally, it was through the interviews rather than the questionnaires that a greater historical perspective was obtained. For example, many parents raising young children today did seem to feel differently about the play than did parents raising children of the same age even five years ago, and many parents believed that their children's war play was different in nature and scope than the war play they themselves engaged in when they were children.

DATA FROM TEACHERS AND OTHER EARLY-CHILDHOOD PROFESSIONALS

While sixteen teachers at three daycare centers completed questionnaires, we ended up relying heavily on interview data with teachers because of the rich and varied information that the interviews seemed to provide. A total of forty-two adults who are professionally involved with children were interviewed, including (in overlapping categories) thirty-five teachers who taught children ranging in age from two to ten years (most from three to six years), five school directors, five early-childhood teacher educators, four teachers who had been in the field for over twenty years and two for over forty years, three child therapists, one pediatrician, and two toy designers. While a large number of the interviews were with Massachusetts residents, such other locations as California, Illinois, Colorado, and Texas were also represented. At least half of the interviews were conducted with people whom it was known in advance had concerns about children's current war play; they expressed concern in advance, and we interviewed them in order to gain as full an understanding as possible of the nature of early-childhood professionals' current concerns about war play. For the other half of the sample, as well as for the respondents of the questionnaires, attitudes toward war play were not known in advance.

From the sixteen questionnaires completed by teachers, some interesting patterns emerged. All of the teachers reported that the children in their classrooms attempted to engage in war and weapons play. All noted sex differences, namely, that boys were much more commonly involved than girls. Of the teachers who described the play in some detail, all but one mentioned the influence of television. With respect to teachers' responses to the play, most attempted to ban the play, usually in the form of a "no guns in school" rule. Two-thirds of the teachers expressed dissatisfaction with their current approach to the play.

Because of the biased nature of the sample and the open-ended nature of the interviews, we did not try to quantify the responses. In general, the interview responses reflected similar patterns to those reported in the questionnaires. What also came out of these interviews was a series of themes that have been discussed throughout this book, such as

- How children meet their needs through war play and what they might be learning from it
- How children's war play has been changing and classroom issues that arise from this
- The changing influence of the television and toy industries on children's play and learning
- Confusion over what role(s) to take with respect to war play in the classroom
- The responsibility of educators with respect to the play and the political socialization of children

We have used the information from these interviews to organize our thinking about war play and as a basis for our own investigation of this topic. We began to formulate our ideas out of concerns expressed by teachers; through our continuing dialogues with them, we continued to refine our thinking.

DATA FROM CHILDREN

The questions in the child-interview form were used to guide discussions with children about their war play. Ten children, ranging in age from three to sixteen years of age (seven were under six years), were interviewed in depth. Many other briefer discussions were conducted with children; these included some but not all of the questions listed on the following form. These briefer discussions generally focused on and immediately followed specific observations of the children as they engaged in war play or used war toys, and the questions asked were related to the children's thinking about that specific play situation. The results of the interviews and observations served to supplement the information we obtained from teachers and parents, as well as to assist in the formulation of the guidelines for actively working with war play.

Parent Questionnaire

Name of child (optional) _____

Age of child _____   Sex of child _____

Age & sex of siblings _____

School _____

1. Does your child engage in war and superhero play?
   IF YES, GO TO QUESTION 3.
   IF NO, ANSWER QUESTION 2.

2. IF NO:

   (a) Do you feel this is due to lack of interest on your child's part or to some other reasons?

   (b) What would you do if your child attempted to engage in this play?

   (c) If your child watches TV cartoons, which ones are his or her favorites?

   (d) Is there anything else you would like to tell us about this topic?

   THANK YOU. PLEASE STOP HERE & RETURN QUESTIONNAIRE TO YOUR CHILD'S SCHOOL.

3. IF YES:

   (a) Can you please describe the war and superhero play?

   (b) Does your child use guns, war toys, or other props? (If yes, what kinds; e.g., real, fingers, blocks, commercial, toys, costumes, etc.?)

   (c) What are the themes/characters in the play?

   (d) If your child watches TV cartoons, which are his or her favorites?

(e) Do you see themes and characters from TV in your child's play? If yes, please describe.

(f) Can you remember when and how your child's interest was first expressed?

(g) How do you feel about this play?

(h) How do you respond to your child's play (i.e., do you take any role)?

(i) Is there anything else you would like to tell us about this topic?

Teacher Questionnaire

School _____

Respondent's Name (optional) _____

Age of Children _____   Size of Classroom _____

Type of Setting (e.g., nursery school, public school, daycare): _____

Length of time teaching _____ years.

1. Have the children in your classroom ATTEMPTED to engage in war and weapons play?

2. If NO, please go to QUESTION #6.

3. If YES, how do you respond?

4. If you ban this play,

    (a) How do you ban it?

    (b) What do you say?

    (c) How do you feel about this approach?

5. If you respond by permitting war and weapons play,

    (a) Under what circumstances? (e.g., any limits? ground rules? your role? etc.)

    (b) What general themes come up in the play?

    (c) Can you briefly describe the play?

    (d) Have you noticed sex differences in relation to this play? If yes, please describe.

    (e) How do you feel about your approach?

    (f) If you have taught more than 4 years, do you see any changes in children's war and weapons play during your years as a teacher?

6. Is there anything else you would like to tell us about this topic?

Child Interview

Questions to begin discussion:

1. Do you play any good-guy/bad-guy games like G.I. Joe, Superheroes, etc? (Probe for war play and concepts about it.)

2. Do you watch television? (Probe for ideas about war-related TV and relationship to play.)

3. Tell me about what G.I. Joe (other character mentioned) does in your play. (Probe for how closely character matches TV script.)

4. Could G.I. Joe (other character) come into this class? Is he real? Where do you think you could find him? (Probe for concepts of real and pretend.)

5. What happens when G.I. Joe (other character) shoots somebody? (Probe for effects of violent acts.)

6. Have you ever heard of Russians or Germans or any people like that? What do you know about them? (Probe for concept of enemy in the real world.)

7. What is an enemy? (Probe for concept of enemy and mix of pretend and real.)

8. Do you ever fight or disagree with your friend? What would G.I. Joe (other character) do if he were in that fight? (Probe for concepts about conflict resolution and real in relation to pretend.)

9. (Other questions to pursue child's interests.)

APPENDIX II

Two Sample Curriculum Webs

In this appendix we present two sample curriculum webs, one using *The Wizard of Oz*[1] and the other developing themes around children's play focused on creatures from outer space.

Such curriculum webs can be useful to teachers in a number of ways. They can assist teachers in keeping track of activities that occur as well as in planning what might happen next (Levin, 1986). They provide a technique for quickly recording and organizing a great deal of information about a classroom in a visually clear and easy-to-read fashion. No two webs will ever look the same; the information in the web will depend on the particular setting, and the categories used and connections made among categories will depend on the reason and functions of the web. For example, a web may be used to record information about what has occurred around a theme, around subject areas, or around teacher interventions; to plan for a new theme; to further activities that have already occurred; to plan for one child, based on what she or he has already done. Weaving webs on a regular basis (e.g., weekly, or at the beginning, middle, and end of a particular theme) can provide systematic documentation of the curriculum as well as a regular procedure for curriculum development. Teachers might work together in making webs; in such a case, the web making provides a way to share information quickly that each teacher obtained and to plan for shared objectives and responses. Teachers might share their webs with parents, to give an overview of what has been occurring in the classroom related to war play, as well as the range of activities, learning, and issues that might have been involved. The process of making a curriculum web is usually as important as the product obtained, because of the organizing of information that occurs as it is made. The first few attempted are often the most difficult because it can be difficult at first to brainstorm in a free and nonlinear

---

[1]Many of the curriculum ideas for the curriculum web on *The Wizard of Oz* came from Martha Eshoo.

manner, thus breaking away from the more familiar approach of organizing information in a linear and logical fashion (e.g., a series of lessons).

The following two curriculum webs will illustrate these points.

Curriculum Web of Ideas for Activities around a Book: *The Wizard of Oz*

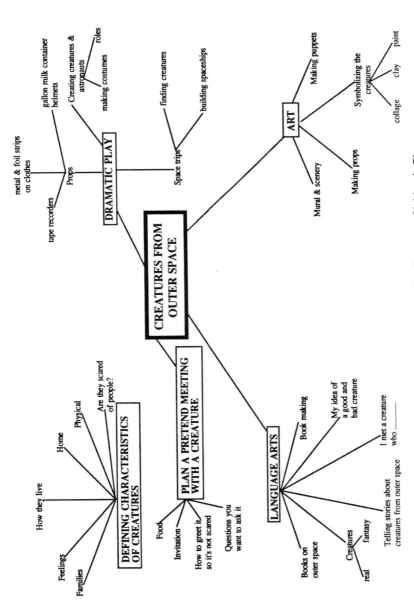

Curriculum Web Developing Activities around a Theme in Children's Play

DRAMATIC PLAY

Props
- metal & foil strips on clothes
- tape recorders
- gallon milk container helmets

Creating creatures & astronauts
- roles
- making costumes

Space trips
- finding creatures
- building spaceships

CREATURES FROM OUTER SPACE

ART

Making puppets

Symbolizing the creatures
- collage
- clay
- paint

Mural & scenery

Making props

DEFINING CHARACTERISTICS OF CREATURES

- How they live
- Home
- Physical
- Are they scared of people?
- Feelings
- Families
- Food

PLAN A PRETEND MEETING WITH A CREATURE

- Invitation
- How to greet it so it's not scared
- Questions you want to ask it

LANGUAGE ARTS

- Book making
- My idea of a good and bad creature
- I met a creature who ....
- Telling stories about creatures from outer space
- Creatures
  - real
  - fantasy
- Books on outer space

Two Record-Keeping Formats

Standardizing the forms used to gather observations is a good way to ensure that data are collected systematically and organized in a readily usable fashion. Making up and reproducing a form like the one shown in Figure A.1 can simplify recording and analyzing information on children's play behavior. It is helpful to arrange the chart so that arrows can be drawn between the names of children who play together; lines can also be used to link an observation to more than one name, thus minimizing repetition on the form. Information can be recorded during the day as the teacher makes observations, or at the end of the day. Because each child's box is always in the same place, the teacher can easily retrieve information about a given child by flipping through the accumulated pages.

It is up to the teacher to decide what kind of data to collect. Possibilities include: children's involvement in war-related play, extensions that arise in the play, experiences with conflict resolution, and discussions about war-play-related issues. Teachers can also make notes to themselves about patterns and needs that emerge for individual children and about issues to work on next.

The form shown in Figure A.2 can be thought of as somewhat equivalent to lesson planning and evaluation. A second page containing columns for Thursday, Friday, and a weekly summary should be placed opposite the Monday-Wednesday page so that the whole week can be seen at once. The teacher can fill out the appropriate column each night, both recording what happened on a given day and also planning for the next day. At the end of the week, the teachers can reflect back and record summary comments and future goals in the sixth column.

Class List: Date:

Alice	Natasha	Kelly
Wanda	James	Mary
Marcus	Luisa	Maya
Emile	Joseph	Miguel
Henry	Casey	Julio

Figure A.1   Sample Format for Keeping Records on Individual Children

Monday	Tuesday	Wednesday
PLANS:	PLANS:	PLANS:
WHAT HAPPENED:	WHAT HAPPENED:	WHAT HAPPENED:

Figure A.2   Sample Format for Keeping Records on the Curriculum

Annotated List of Organizations Working on Peace Education and War Toy Issues

ACTION FOR CHILDREN'S TELEVISION (ACT)
46 Austin Street, Newtonville, MA 02160
(617) 527-7870
> Distributes a newsletter, books and pamphlets, films, and other materials, including a speaker's kit and television viewing guide for children.

CONCERNED EDUCATORS ALLIED FOR A SAFE ENVIRON-
MENT (CEASE)
c/o Peggy Schirmer, 17 Gerry Street, Cambridge, MA 02138
> National network of parents and teachers of young children working to educate themselves and the public about global issues. Currently focusing on antiwar-toys efforts nationwide. Distributes quarterly newsletter. Membership organization ($5/year).

EDUCATORS FOR SOCIAL RESPONSIBILITY (ESR)
23 Garden Street, Cambridge, MA 02138
(617) 492-1764
> Works with educators, students, and parents to introduce war and peace curriculum into school systems. Produces and distributes several detailed curriculum guides on peace education issues (kindergarten through high school). Sponsors conferences and provides speakers. Membership organization; local and national chapters ($20/year).

NATIONAL ASSOCIATION FOR THE EDUCATION OF YOUNG CHILDREN (NAEYC)
1834 Connecticut Ave. NW, Washington, DC 20009
(202) 232-8777; (800) 424-2460

Provides many resources, including books, pamphlets, posters, and a journal (*Young Children*). Local and state chapters, national conference. Membership organization (price varies with local chapters).

NATIONAL COALITION ON TELEVISION VIOLENCE (NCTV)
P.O. Box 2157, Champaign, IL 61820
(217) 384-1920

Monitors television violence (especially as it relates to children's programming), sends out periodic reports and press releases, produces a regular newsletter. Membership organization ($25/year).

UNITARIAN UNIVERSALIST SERVICE COMMITTEE (Boston Area Unit)
78 Beacon Street, Boston, MA 02108
(617) 742-2120

Working on antiwar-toy activities. Distributes periodic newsletter. Member of the Unitarian Universalist Association Peace Network.

WAR RESISTERS LEAGUE/NEW ENGLAND (WRL)
P.O. Box 1093, Norwich, CT 06360
(203) 889-5337

Involved in an international effort to limit the proliferation of war toys. Distributes a Stop War Toys Campaign Packet ($4) and "War Toys on the March" leaflet; provides speakers on war toys; serves as a clearinghouse for groups in the U.S. doing work against war toys.

References

Althea. (1975). *Desmond and the monsters*. Cambridge, England: Dinosaur Publications.

Balaban, N. (1985). *Starting school: From separation to independence*. New York: Teachers College Press.

Baum, L. F. (1979). *The wizard of Oz*. New York: Ballantine Books.

Bettelheim, B. (1967). Children should learn about violence. *The Saturday Evening Post, 240*(10), pp. 10, 12.

Biber, B., Murphy, L. B., Woodcock, L. P., & Black, I. S. (1942). *Child life in school: A study of a seven-year-old group*. New York: E. P. Dutton.

Boyer, P. J. (1986, February 3). Toy-based TV: Effects on children debated. *New York Times*, pp. A1, C22.

Bruner, J. S. (1960). *The process of education*. New York: Vintage Books.

Carlsson-Paige, N., & Levin, D. E. (1985). *Helping young children understand peace, war and the nuclear threat*. Washington, DC: National Association for the Education of Young Children.

Carlsson-Paige, N., & Levin D. E. (1986). "The Butter Battle Book": Uses and abuses with young children. *Young Children, 41*(3), 37–42.

Chodorow, N. (1978). *The reproduction of mothering*. Berkeley, CA: University of California Press.

Cohen, D. (1974). Is TV a pied piper? *Young Children, 30*(1), 4–14.

Coles, R. (1986a). *The moral life of children*. Boston: The Atlantic Monthly Press.

Coles, R. (1986b). *The political life of children*. Boston: The Atlantic Monthly Press.

Davis, G. (1976). *Childhood and history in America*. New York: The Psychohistory Press.

Dawson, R. E., & Prewitt, K. (1969). *Political socialization*. Boston: Little, Brown.

Denison, D. C. (1985, December 8). The year of playing dangerously. *The Boston Globe Magazine*, pp. 14–16, 99–107, 110.

Doerkin, M. (1983). *Classroom combat, teaching and television*. Englewood Cliffs, NJ: Educational Technology Publications.

Easton, D., & Hess, R. D. (1962). The child's political world. *Midwest Journal of Political Science, 6*, 235–238.

Elkind, D. (1976). *Child development and education: A Piaget perspective.* New York: Oxford University Press.

Elkind, D., Hetzel, D. & Coe, J. (1974). Piaget and British primary education. *Educational Psychologist, 11*(1), 1–10.

Elliot, J. (1976). *Developing hypotheses about classroom from teachers' practical constructs.* Grand Forks, ND: North Dakota Study Group in Evaluation, University of North Dakota.

Engelhardt, T. (1986). Saturday morning fever: The hard sell takeover of kids' TV. *Mother Jones, 11*(6), 38–48, 54.

Erikson, E. H. (1963). Childhood and society. New York: W. W. Norton.

Feinburg, S. G. (1973). *Combat in child art.* New York: W. W. Norton.

Fisher, R. (1981). *Getting to yes.* New York: Penguin Press.

Freud, A., & Burlingham, D. T. (1943). *War and children.* New York: Ernst Willard.

Gibbs, J. C., & Schnell, S. V. (1985). Moral development "versus" socialization. *American Psychologist, 40*(10), 1071–1080.

Gilligan, C. (1982). *In a different voice.* Cambridge, MA: Harvard University Press.

Group for the Advancement of Psychiatry. (1982). *The child and television drama: The psychological impact of cumulative viewing.* New York: Mental Health Materials Center.

Gruber, H. E., & Vonèche, J. J. (Eds.). (1977). *The essential Piaget.* New York: Basic Books.

Heck, S. F., & Williams, C. R. (1984). *The complex roles of the teacher: An ecological perspective.* New York: Teachers College Press.

Hess, R., & Torney, J. (1969). *The development of political attitudes in children.* Chicago: Aldine.

Hohmann, M., Banet, B., & Weikart, D. P. (1979). *Young children in action: A manual for preschool educators.* Ypsilanti, MI: High/Scope Press.

Honig, A. S. (1983). Research review: TV violence and child aggression. *Day Care and Early Education, 10*(4), 41–45.

Isaacs, S. (1937). *Social development in young children.* London: Routledge & Kegan Paul.

Kamii, C., & DeVries, R. (1978). *Physical knowledge in early childhood education: Implications of Piaget's theory.* Englewood Cliffs, NJ: Prentice-Hall.

Kamii, C., & DeVries, R. (1980). *Group games in early education: Implications of Piaget's theory.* Washington, DC: National Association for the Education of Young Children.

Kegan, R. (1982). *The evolving self: Problem and process in human development.* Cambridge, MA: Harvard University Press.

Kohl, H. (1976). *On teaching.* New York: Schocken Books.

Kohlberg, L. (1966). A cognitive-developmental analysis of children's sex-role concepts and attitudes. In E. Maccoby (Ed.), *The development of sex differences* (pp. 82–173). Stanford, CA: Stanford University Press.

Kohlberg, L. (1969). Stage and sequence: The cognitive-developmental approach to socialization. In D. A. Goslin (Ed.), *Handbook of socialization theory and research* (pp. 347–480). New York: Rand McNally.

Kostelnik, M. J., Whiren, A. P., & Stein, L. C. (1986). Living with He-Man: Managing superhero fantasy play. *Young Children, 41*(4), 3–9.

Kriedler, W. (1984). *Creative conflict resolution: More than 200 activities for keeping peace in the classroom.* Glenview, IL: Scott, Foresman.

Levin, D. E. (1986). Weaving curriculum webs: Planning, guiding and recording curriculum activities. *Day Care and Early Education, 13*(4), 16–19.

Lightfoot, S. (1978). *Worlds apart.* Cambridge, MA: Harvard University Press.

Lyons, H. A. (1971). Psychiatric sequelae to the Belfast riot. *British Journal of Psychiatry, 118*(544), 265–273.

MacMaster, C. (1986, March). Are war toys turning the playground into a battlefield? *Whole Life, 49,* 21.

Moore, S. W., Lare, J., & Wagner, K. A. (1985). *The child's political world: A longitudinal perspective.* New York: Praeger.

Neumann, E. A. (1971). *The elements of play.* New York: MSS Information Corporation.

Orwell, G. (1946). *Boys' Weeklies: A collection of essays.* San Diego, CA: Harcourt, Brace, Jovanovich.

Owen, D. (1986). Where toys come from. *The Atlantic Monthly, 258*(4), 65–78.

Paley, V. G. (1984). *Boys and girls: Superheroes in the doll corner.* Chicago: University of Chicago Press.

Philadelphia Teachers' Learning Cooperative. (1984). On becoming teacher experts: Buying time. *Language Arts, 61*(71), 731–736.

Piaget, J. (1951). *Play, dreams, and imitation in childhood.* New York: W. W. Norton. (Original French edition published 1945)

Piaget, J. (1965). *The moral judgement of the child.* New York: Free Press. (Original French edition published 1932)

Piaget, J. (1973). *To understand is to invent: The future of education.* New York: Grossman Publishers.

Piaget, J., & Inhelder, B. (1969). *The psychology of the child.* New York: Basic Books. (Original French edition published 1966)

Piaget, J., & Weil, A. M. (1951). The development in children of the idea of the homeland and of relations with other countries. *International Social Science Bulletin, 3,* 561–578.

Pitcher, E. G., & Prelinger, E. (1969). *Children tell stories.* New York: International Universities Press.

Raposa, L. (1986, March 22). The toy market is transformed. *The Boston Herald,* pp. 28–29.

Rudolph, M., & Cohen, D. H. (1984). *Kindergarten and early schooling* (2nd ed.). Englewood Cliffs, NJ: Prentice-Hall.

Sadker, M., & Sadker, D. (1985, March). Sexism in the schoolroom of the eighties. *Psychology Today,* pp. 54–57.

Schneiderman, J., & Sousa, C. (1986). Superheroes in the preschool classroom. *Child Care News, 12*(9), 1, 4, & 5.

Seefeldt, C., & Tinney, S. (1985). Dinosaurs: The past is present. *Young Children, 40*(4), 20–24.

Segaloff, N. (1986, March 23). "Battle of Rock Lords" a lost cause. *The Boston Herald*, pp. 28–29.

Sendak, M. (1963). *Where the wild things are*. New York: Harper & Row.

Simpson, C. (1985). The violence of war toys: He-Man, Voltron, Transformers, and Gobots. *The Nonviolent, 2*(8), 3–4, 6.

Singer, D. G. (1983). A time to reexamine the role of television in our lives. *American Psychologist, 38*(7), 815–816.

Singer, D. G., & Singer, J. L. (1981a). Raising boys who know how to love. In R. D. Strom (Ed.), *Growing through play: Readings for parents and teachers*. Monterey, CA: Brooks Cole.

Singer, J. L., & Singer, D. G. (1981b). *Television, imagination and aggression: A study of preschoolers*. Hillsdale, NJ: Lawrence Erlbaum Associates.

Singer, D. G., & Singer, J. L. (1984). TV violence: What's all the fuss about? *Television and Children, 7*(2), 30–41.

Smilansky, S. (1968). *The effects of sociodramatic play on disadvantaged preschool children*. New York: John Wiley.

Smilansky, S. (1971). Can adults facilitate play in children? Theoretical and practical considerations. In N. E. Curry & S. Arnaud (Eds.), *Play: The child strives toward self-realization*. Washington, DC: National Association for the Education of Young Children.

Sutton-Smith, B., & Roberts, J. M. (1981). In H. C. Triandis & A. Heron (Eds.), *Handbook of cross-cultural psychology* (Vol. 4, pp. 425–471). Boston: Allyn and Bacon.

Swedish Information Service. (1980, September). War toys. *Social Change in Sweden*, No. 19, p. 5.

Torney-Purta, J. (1984). Political socialization and policy: The United States in a cross-national context. In H. W. Stevenson & A. E. Siegel (Eds.), *Child development research and social policy* (Vol. 1, pp. 471–523). Chicago: University of Chicago Press.

White, R. (1959). Motivation reconsidered: The concept of competence. *Psychological Review, 66*(5), 297–333.

Wilson, B. R. (1975). The teacher's role: A sociological analysis. In H. R. Stub (Ed.), *The sociology of education: A sourcebook* (3rd ed., pp. 309–326). Homewood, IL: The Dorsey Press.

Winn, M. (1983). *Children without childhood*. New York: Pantheon Books.

Winn, M. (1985). *The plug-in drug: Television, children and the family*. New York: Penguin Books.

Witkowsky, K. (1986). Up in arms over guns in toyland. *Mother Jones, 11*(3), 12.

Wolf, D. P. (1984). Superheroes: Yes or no?: An interview with Carolee Fucigna and Michelle Heist. *Beginnings, 1*(1), 29–32.

Wolf, D. P. (1986). Who cares? Reexamining the context of children's friendship: An interview with Nancy Carlsson-Paige and Diane Levin. In D. P.

Wolf (Ed.), *Connecting: Friendship in the lives of young children and their teachers* (pp. 110–118). Redmond, WA: Exchange Press.

Wyner, N. (1978). Children becoming citizens. In A. L. Pagano (Ed.), *Social studies in early childhood: An interactionist point of view* (pp. 40–54). Washington, DC: National Council for the Social Studies.

Index

Engelhardt, T., 2, 13, 14, 29
Erikson, E. H., 18

Fantasy, 55
  boundary between reality and, 18–20
  political concepts and, 27
Federal Communications Commission
    (FCC), 13–14, 74
Federal Trade Commission, 74
Feinberg, S. G., 2
Finland, 74–75
Fisher, R., 70
Folklore, 59
Freud, A., 28

Gender, 32
  war play and, 21–22, 65–69
Gibbs, J. C., 34
G. I. Joe, 1, 2n., 9, 14, 27–28, 56, 63
Gilligan, C., 22
Girls, 21–22, 65
Government by law, 25
Group for the Advancement of
    Psychiatry, 13
Gruber, H. E., 23
Guilt, 45, 61

Heck, S. F., 69
He-Man, 1, 2n., 15, 27, 39–40,
    67–68
Hess, R., 24
Hess, R. D., 24
Hetzel, D., 59
Hohmann, M., 56, 59
Honig, A. S., 15, 29

Images in play, 54
Imitation, 22–23, 35–36, 55
Impulse control, 18, 20–21, 60–61
Inhelder, B., 18
Interviews
  of children, 83, 87
  of parents, 80–81
  of teachers, 82–83
Isaacs, S., 17, 18, 35, 53, 60

Kamii, C., 18, 25, 53, 54, 57
Kegan, R., 18
Kohl, H., 58, 60
Kohlberg, L., 21, 34

Kostelnik, M. J., 2, 4, 18, 45, 60
Kriedler, W., 58

Lare, J., 24
Legos, 63, 64
Levin, D. E., 19, 20, 26, 28, 34, 53, 58, 89
Lightfoot, S., 50
Literature, 59
Lyons, H. A., 28

Macho attributes, 21
MacMaster, C., 2
Masters of the Universe, 15, 39–41
Militarism
  in animated television shows, 29–32
  defined, 4n.
  in nuclear age, 15–16
  war play and, 32–36
Misogyny, 32
Moore, S. W., 24
Murphy, L. B., 2

National Association for the Education
    of Young Children (NAEYC), 98
National Coalition on Television
    Violence (NCTV), 14, 98
Neumann, E. A., 18
Nuclear age, 15–16
  play based on, 28

Open-ended questions, 56–57
Owen, D., 14

Paley, V. G., 21, 57, 60, 61, 65, 67, 68
Parents
  approaches of, compared to teachers,
    50–51
  dialog with teachers, 70–71
  interview data from, 80–81
  questionnaire data from, 79–80, 84–85
  tensions with children, 8–11
Peer group pressure, 9
Philadelphia Teachers' Learning
    Cooperative, 69
Piaget, J., 17, 18, 22–23, 25, 35
Pitcher, E. G., 2
Play
  changes in patterns of, 11–12
  purpose of, 35
  sex roles in, 65–69